The Christian and Other Religion

MOWBRAYS LIBRARY OF THEOLOGY

Series Editor: Michael Perry

The Christian and Other Religion

The measure of Christ

Kenneth Cragg

MOWBRAYS LONDON & OXFORD

First Published 1977
by A. R. Mowbray & Co. Ltd
The Alden Press, Osney Mead
Oxford OX2 0EG

ISBN   0 264 66256 3 paper
         0 264 66413 2 cased

Printed in Great Britain
at the Alden Press, Oxford

.

Introduction to Mowbrays Library of Theology

THE last quarter of the twentieth century is a good time for the Christian Church to take stock of its beliefs. In the course of the century, Christian theology has had many challenges to meet—and has itself not remained unchanged by the encounter. Society has become more pluralist and less committed; dogmatism is at a discount. Christianity has had to survive in a climate which regards its beliefs as matters of opinion rather than of fact, and in a world not readily convinced of their relevance either to public politics or private morals. Within the faith (and particularly in the sixties of the century) there have been radical questionings of almost every aspect of doctrine.

Despite all this, there are signs that people are more willing now than they were a decade or so ago to listen to more constructive voices. Christians need to state how they can—as men of their age and culture, and as heirs to the radical ferment of ideas which characterised the mid-century—articulate a faith in God, Father, Son and Holy Spirit, hold convictions about the nature of man and his destiny, and show the relevance of belief to conduct. The contributors to this series think it their duty to give as plain and straightforward a statement as is compatible with their intellectual integrity of what the Christian faith is, and how it can be honestly and meaningfully expressed today.

Christian faith has always been the faith of a community. It is therefore necessary to 'earth' such an articulation in terms of a particular community of Christians. So the contributors to this series are all Anglicans, confident that theirs is a particular expression of the universal faith which still merits serious consideration. The series therefore aims to reflect, not only themes of interest to all Christians at all times, but also particular aspects of Christian theology which are currently exercising the Church of England in congregations and Synods. And, since there will always be rival religions and ideologies competing for men's allegiance, we need to explore their claims and ask what the attitude of Anglicans is towards them. But that the Church has a faith which is worth stating and that it is a faith to live by, is a conviction shared by every contributor.

Michael Perry

Acknowledgements

THE author and publisher wish to acknowledge with gratitude publishers' permission to quote from works under copyright, as follows:

The British Council of Churches, for passages from Bishop David Brown's *A New Threshold* London, 1976), quoted on pp. 73–74.

The Literary Trustees of Walter de la Mare, and the Society of Authors as their representative, for the passage on p. 37 from the *Collected Poems* of Walter de la Mare (London, 1969).

To Messrs Faber & Faber for two extracts from Dag Hammarskjöld's *Markings* (New York, 1964), on pp. 7, 117, 118.

Longman Group Ltd, Harlow, for sentences from S. H. Nasr's *Islam and the Plight of Modern Man* (London, 1976), on p. 85.

Lutterworth Press Ltd, Guildford, for some lines from Hendrik Kraemer's *World Cultures and World Religions* (London, 1960), on pp. 71, 72.

MacGibbon & Kee Ltd, Granada Publishing Co. Ltd, for an extract from Peter Brook's *The Empty Space* (London, 1968) on p. 51.

The Society for Promoting Christian Knowledge, London, for extracts on p. 108, p. 109 from the Doctrine Commission of the Church of England's Report, *Christian Believing* (London, 1976).

Pantheon Books Ltd, for the passages on p. 18 from Mai Mai Sze's *The Tao of Painting* (Bollinger series, xlix, 1956).

Eyre Methuen, London, for the extract from Martin Esslin's *The Theatre of the Absurd* (London, 1966), quoted on p. 13.

Contents

Preface

'... CHESS, Church, Court ...'. So run the items in the front-page index of *The Times*, arranged by the alphabet for the convenience of readers. The Christian institution and, by implication, the Christ within it, listed, as it might be a Golf Club or a philatelic hobby, with other jostling activities of life. What claims to be final and conclusive rubs shoulder, by the accident of alphabet, in the competition for popular interest or neglect. Such are the ways of the secular world. The Christian cannot assume that relevance and recognition are in any way commensurate. We offer the indispensable to the unconcerned. At best the Good News seems marginally newsworthy.

The questions deepen if we compile another list—Buddha, Christ, Krishna, Muhammad, Zoroaster. The last, perhaps, is only history. But the others are in actual catalogue with 'the prince of glory' of our devotion, with 'the Lord from heaven' of our theology. How then should faith in him relate to the pluralism of religious man? What should be our measure of these alternative figures in the history and the making of the world's religions? They are certainly alternative in the considerable sense that they are other guides than ours to life and meaning, though the faiths that cluster round them have not, for the most part, been options freely chosen out of a feasible neutrality, but rather denominators of birth and culture, of language and geography.

Our Christian co-existence with them in the contemporary world raises sharp questions both for theology and for pastoral activity. Other religions are no longer—if they ever were—remote and academic factors in a world-picture which the ordinary Christian could ignore. In the day of Asian and African nationhood they have a living, if indeterminate, role in world affairs. They belong with massive and multiplying populations of mankind. Further, their adherents are in our own midst, immigrant and other communities side by side with us in local residence, sharing our schools, needing our facilities, circulating among us. These bring the problems of interreligion—if we may so speak—right into the life and thinking of our parishes.

This book does not aim to describe and assess the major faiths. It takes its place in a 'Library of Theology', in the conviction that a Christian relation with them is a primary task both of reflection and responsibility. The chapters that follow include serious areas of the thought and expression of other faiths, but move always in the context of concern for Christian relationship. They can hope, therefore, to be informative in the prior aim to be relational. Exposition of Buddhist, Hindu, Muslim, or other, doctrines is seen as contributory to exploring the dimensions of Christian obligation. The question: What do they teach? is not isolated from the kindred issue: How do we, how may we, respond?

Correspondingly, the relevant interior Christian themes of finality, authority, truth, mission and ministry, are not to be handled only from within. In every case they must be set in the active sphere of attention to the other, of mutual openness and reckoning. Abstract comparison or theological theory alone, whether dogmatic or sentimental, are no adequate relation to what is involved. The art of loyalty and the art of relationship must be understood, and practised, as complementary.

In the main title 'Christian' is, of course, the noun and not the adjective, the person not the classification. The book is an attempt to help the Christian to be one, in terms both of thinking and of action. The title, too, speaks of 'religion' deliberately in the singular, looking for the living commitment, our own and that of others, beyond the formal category, the heart rather than the system. 'Religions', in the plural, suggest a more institutionalised, formal, even external, quantity, where personal engagement may be lost to sight or shrunk into a label. In his *The Meaning and End of Religion*, Wilfred Cantwell Smith has insisted that 'there are Hindus but no Hinduism'.[1] The dictum is too sharp, since one has presumably to identify Hindus by their Hinduism. The '-ism' has its claim on our concern, diffused as it may be in a multitude of people, in whom it only exists as *their* religiousness. We still have to think of 'continuing traditions', or some such phrase, if we choose to disallow the other usage. Here, by the word in the singular, it is intended to emphasise that we have to do with felt and lived religious meaning, rather than with its abstraction into '-ism'.

As for religionlessness, that, on reflection, is all the time within religion. In disavowing 'religions' as crutches for cripples, or excuses for evaders, or for any other reason, one is simply requiring truer religion. All the articulate reasons for irreligion are essentially religious.

The sub-title sets the central chapter as the clue to the whole and is only not preferred to the main title for publishing considerations. The Christian's point of departure and of return is always 'God in Christ'. For his criterion is there, both of truth and of relationship.

Chapter 1, borrowing the title of a recent novel out of Ghana, makes certain general points about the contemporary world and its human community. The earth is our common space ship and, beyond all religious plurals, is the single territory of our humanness. We have to begin, so to speak, with the selfness of our selfhood, with man as the existential subject of all religious meaning.

Chapter 2, on the right courtesies, in advance of any detailed issues, tries to plead the case of reverence for reverence and the need to penetrate faiths as their insiders know them, if there is to be hope of reciprocal awareness. This does not mean a sentimentality oblivious of the compromises or the crimes of which religions have been guilty. But realism has its positive duties, too, and the first of these is a hospitable mind.

In Chapter 3 an attempt is made to set the dimensions of religion, as the Semitic theisms see them, and then to take them in the contrasted verdict of the Asian monisms. By those contrasts and kinships of soul the discussion can move into the whole secular critique of both broad streams of religious existence.

As a *confessio fidei*, Chapter 4 aims to define the Christian by his position within the first stream, seeing his distinctive theism alongside the variant emphases that identify his Judaic and Islamic neighbours. The whole exposition, rather like the Isaian: 'Who hath believed our report?' must be open to the sceptical, as that which may well have in its interrogatives the very measure by which we would be understood in our affirmatives.

With these canons of reckoning in mind, we are ready for a parenthesis. Chapter 5 reviews in brief survey some phases and theories of Christian thinking in the field of comparative theology, beginning with C. F. Andrews whose Christian response to India held in tension many of the problems. Barth, Kraemer, Hocking, Toynbee, Hick and David Brown are some of the names that concern us here, with their variant attitudes to the basic question whether exclusive, or inclusive, or both, are the terms in which to state the Gospel of Jesus *vis-à-vis* the faiths in the world. A theology of pluralism and of mission within it is still in the making. We need to take bearings on the story and its likely future.

From that parenthesis we return to two final interdependent chapters, 6 and 7, on the saving mind and the Holy Spirit, resuming the obligations implicit in the *confessio fidei* of Chapter 4. While the treatment throughout is religious, and of religious attitudes and claims, we cannot forget that many ideologies and sciences and philosophies are undertaking to interpret, to organise and to resolve the human situation. Our overriding concern is to care, not for controversies as arenas of *our* victory, not for contention in *their* disproof, but for salvation, for saving, as it were, the very ideas of salvation. Just as the theme of man, rather than religious dogma, seemed the right starting point for our studies, so the presence, the active invocation, of the Holy Spirit, becomes the right reliance and the pledge of hope in their conclusion. For with the Holy Spirit we can well leave every problem, but only in readiness to receive it back again as ours. 'The Holy Spirit and us . . . ' (Acts 15.28) was the apostolic formula at a historic moment, as crucial and decisive as our own, 'the eternal moment which is always now'.

KENNETH CRAGG

The University of Sussex

1 'This Earth, My Brother'

A READER new to the Bhagavad Gita, most loved of the Scriptures of the Hindus, might be forgiven for thinking that, in the opening chapter, there might be a clue to the attraction Asian attitudes hold today for many western minds. For Prince Arjuna, in this 'Song of the Blessed One', sounds remarkably like the would-be drop-out of our time, at odds with the world in which he finds himself and whose conventions he is supposed to follow.

Such a reader would be wrong. For Arjuna is educated out of his first misgiving as the poem proceeds. The final meaning of the Gita is the celebration of disinterested response to the *dharma/karma* of human destiny. Krishna, in the guise of the charioteer, persuades Arjuna's reluctance into action until, his scruples overcome, he yields up his reservations in discipleship.

Yet there remains something authentic about the quality of his beginning. Facing that battle-ground of human society, summoned into combat even against his own kind, expected to assume an officialised existence, Arjuna feels only dismay and disquiet. Absurdity and nausea might be the modern terms.

> As I see them here, my own kinsfolk
> Drawing nearer, so eager to fight,
> My limbs sink down, my throat is parched,
> And there is trembling in my body:
> My bow falls from my hand . . .
> Surely we of ourselves know enough
> To turn back from this wickedness.
> My mind is bewildered . . .

How close he is to our own contemporary alienation. We have heard the same will to exempt themselves in numbers of our generation in poetry and drama.

Is it not here that religion must begin—this earth and this human family? Here are all its human elements—life as a personal dilemma, kinships in the flesh, constraints in society, puzzles in the soul, pressures in the will. The Gita opens in a universal human idiom, with man, mortal, dismayed, alienated, obligated, wistful. It resolves him, after its own pattern, with a firm tuition, reinforced by mingled solace, authority and promise. It decides the self he is to be and schools him to be it. But man, when the Gita opens, is in deep, disquieted interrogation of the world. It is that quality, break and bend it as the poem does, which most commends him to our kindred minds. Even the traditions which have least place for the autonomy of the self have, somehow, to begin there.

Muslim Scripture, like the Bible, starts very differently, with God and with invocation. To begin: 'In the name of God ... ' makes a sharp contrast with: 'On the field of *dharma*, on the battle ground of life ...'. But, either way, man takes the stage. For the drama is about him and within him. Elsewhere in the Qur'an comes a cluster of questions which have the same elemental quality as Arjuna's, except that they are to man and not from him. 'Have you considered the seed you spill? ... Have you considered what you plough? ... Have you considered the water you drink? ... Have you considered the fire you kindle?' Here are basic things—procreation, husbandry, subsistence, technology, life and earth and water and fire. The verb repeated in the questions has both the simple sense of visual, and the reflective sense of valuational, awareness. Man has both to recognise and reckon with what is. All are then solemnised in the cosmic setting: 'Nay! I swear by the courses of the stars—a tremendous invocation, did you but know' (Surah 56.58, 63, 68, 71 and 75–6).[1]

Adjured and interrogated in this way, man stands between sentience and the stars, a self within the world, in the vast, yet intimate, complex of his mortal being and in a chain of contingency which he briefly links by his own existence, precarious yet kingly in his dominion over things.

There is deliberate point in beginning this way from the human end. Some would prefer to start from God and come to man out of a confident theism. In one sense it does not matter either way. For such theology, if it is to be right, must in its implications be properly identifying man, just as a true understanding of the human, if we can reach it, will be a large factor in theological conclusions. Where, however, our primary concern is with the meeting of faiths we have little option but to begin from the human side. Theology, in dogmatic and institutionalised form, is likely to be divisive, perhaps even combative. Some deep religious areas, as, for example, within Buddhism, will be excluded altogether if we proceed from theological premises only, or initially. As reverent theists we can be sure that we shall never be far away from a living theology if we are radically and honestly committed to understanding man. That accent in our thinking will more readily enable the meeting we intend across religious frontiers. For this is the common ground. Here, though no doubt much in dispute, the data are mutually accessible and inwardly known. Whether or not we share the sense of divine grace, we certainly participate in the human condition. It is this alone which allows us the hope of finding ground where all our pluralisms meet.

Here is the common denominator, whatever the diversity of its interpretation in myth or symbol, creed and culture, through all the determining constraints of history and society. In and beneath all manifestations of its nature, the human presence constitutes the religious criterion from which we may begin. Indeed, religion could be said to be the act, or the art, of receiving the human situation in such terms, reading that situation, so to speak, in the original, exploring it in its full dimensions, sensing as partial and so rejecting the attitudes which circumscribe its range of meaning. No doubt religious attitudes themselves have often aided and abetted such partialities of mind, found them convenient or comforting, feared to call them into question and falsely proclaimed them sacrosanct. But the vocation to a loyalty more ultimate than *forms* of religion remains the deepest religious obligation. The proper measure—if we may so speak—of what makes religion truly religious is not in Jacob bargaining at Bethel to make his selfishness secure. It is in Jacob at Peniel, wrestling with the angel for the meaning of his selfhood. The one calculates in 'the house of God', even in his dreams; the other yearns for the truth of himself before 'the face of God'.

It will be asked by some whether this human point of departure for our relating of the religions is not unduly assuming the human significance. A cosmic illusionist will see it as altogether pretentious. Should we not reject the extravagance of taking the cue so proudly from ourselves? Do we not need, in this sphere of the total, the same sort of agnosticism Kant taught in the sphere of the empirical, namely that the conditions of our knowing and thinking so determine what we know that we have no right to suppose that things in our knowing correspond to what they are apart from our knowing? By our apparatus of knowing, we phenomenalise, or make phenomena of, what we know. To realise this is to preclude the right to make statements about things outside our acts of comprehension. These are, in Kant's terminology, noumena, and as such are reserved from all knowability beyond that of realising they can never be phenomena. Similarly, what religions formulate is merely human view-pointing with no proper claim to be more than such. This opinion, whether in the Asian form of illusoriness, or in the modern form of philosophic secular scepticism, can offer itself as a more modest humanism than a confident theology.

If, agreeing to begin with the human, we encounter this radical contrast, we do well to face it squarely. Doing so, we have to ask whether this apparent modesty is not in fact false to the situation. If man, in this way, must rule himself irrelevant to ultimate mystery and meaning, then these, in turn, are in no way relevant to him. Far from being properly cautious about them, we would not even be cognisant at all. There is no meaning in deity, or reality, or the transcendent, that is not meaning for man. Irrelevance equals non-reality. True, we may unwarrantably project our human criteria on to mystery. But if they are inherently inappropriate the mystery itself would never emerge to concern our attention, still less our reservations of modesty. The humility proves to be a pseudo thing. To find man's religious experience no feasible clue to its content of reference is to evacuate that experience itself and is certainly, for all human purposes, to opt out of this world.

In this light, any repudiation of the task of religion means, in effect, the self-repudiation of man. Faith, and the faiths, have to do with the transcendent reference of self-consciousness. As Louis Duprée has it: 'The person is sacred; therefore the sacred *is*.'[2] Aspects of all the foregoing will develop in Chapter 3 below: the immediate purpose is to sustain the decision to move from within the human as in no way invalid for a wise theology and certainly as a congenial proceeding for faiths, both theological and otherwise, intending to converse.

To be in religious measure of man, then, is to return to the questions of Arjuna, the questions to Quranic man. It is to return to John Keats's 'vale of soul-making' as the nature of this world. It is to emerge with the Buddha from a sheltered immunity, whether of circumstance or mind, to encounter man, to find him old, to see him sick, to ponder him a corpse, and so to muse on the meaning of his finitude. It is to do all these things in the immediate context of the contemporary scene.

There is no need here to rehearse all the familiar features of a *This Earth, My Brother* theme.[3] Critical analysts and commentaries on the current scene are plentiful enough. Rather let us reflect, for their interreligious significance, on five broad aspects of our situation, which might be described as the compound interest of human history, the conscious pluralisms of culture and religion, the psychic preoccupations characteristic of our time, the retreat from religious assurance, and, finally, the perennial argument between change and hope. With this sort of agenda for description and review, this chapter may aim to provide a right frame of fact for all that has to follow by way of theology or decision.

Compound interest may be a cryptic phrase with which to come to recent history. But our 'present discontents', if we so describe them, proceed from our present destinations and both from the shaping of the past. In this last quarter of the twentieth century, experience seems to have brought us to a new sharpness of the old dilemma between man in his competence and man in his confusion. The fruits of the amenability of nature to man in technology were never more ample, his alienation within them never more stressful and perplexing. Every new power of men is a new power over man, each instalment of scientific attainment a new element in social complexity. Problems have come to have a global size and admit of no escape into an indifferent security. They press from all sides—global imbalance of wealth and resources, global weight of population growth, global issues of environmental exploitation and pollution, and a global balance of nuclear destruction. All these are compounded dividends from the investments of our history, politically in nation states, structurally in capitalist economies and the communist counter-system, concretely in endless urbanisation, all felt bewilderingly within the inner psyche, where finally, if at all, the solutions must arise. Pollution necessitates 'an earth watch', set up at the Stockholm Conference in 1972, to monitor the seas and shores. But how can we effectively monitor and preserve the soul of habitation, the human within the cosmos? What is the ecology which can secure the inner city of the heart? The arts and the artists who might be thought to be its custodians for the most part only reflect the symptoms and confirm the discontents.

The situation is endlessly reported. In an odd way, it is perhaps the very welter of diagnosis that most betrays its chronic character. 'Simplify me .'. .' might well be the sort of plea to which we are driven, and 'simplify society . . .'. Yet simplification is the one thing that eludes us and we know that, could we find it, the price would mean evasion or a false immunity. Our deep need over all—and certainly for any significant converse between faiths—is truly to take, and feel, the measure of the paradox of man, his mastery and misery, and to live in its double quality of achievement and tribulation.

Imagination, in this context, can perhaps best symbolise its task by pondering the expression Dag Hammarskjöld gave it in conceiving a chapel of meditation for the United Nations Headquarters in New York. In a room 'dedicated to silence' a shaft of light strikes the surface of a solid block of iron ore, its meaning clear to all without language. From iron, men have forged their swords, but also reared their cities. So the necessity of choice between destruction and construction is represented in its elemental form under the light which 'daily gives life to the earth on which we stand'. Iron, which incidentally has a Surah to itself in the Qur'an, affords not only the stuff of ploughshares and weapons, but also, in the words of John Ruskin, 'mingles so delicately in our human life that we cannot even blush without its help'.[4] Thus, in Hammarskjöld's mind, an altar, so to speak, of unworked ore of iron could stand, eloquently yet anonymously, in a liturgically neutral silence, relying on nothing but the light of day.

That focus was his attempt to give architectural form to a spirituality, within the United Nations, that did not commit itself unilaterally to any one religion but had, instead, to belong with all in an enterprise whose charter made no mention of God.

People of many faiths will meet here and for that reason none of the symbols to which we are accustomed in our meditation could be used. However, there are simple things which speak to us all in the same language. We have sought for such things and believe that we have found them.[5]

For some, those constraints might have excluded all possible spirituality. But so to conclude would have been to betray the pursuit of peace itself. The way the Christian Dag Hammarskjöld understood his secretary-generalship has within itself a clue for every Christian whose sense of things has obligated him to the pluralism of the world.

This has brought us to our second main reflection in this chapter—the conscious cohabitation of religions and cultures. Pluralisms, of course, there have always been. Climatic, ethnic, tribal, traditional, local, diversities have always characterised the human scene as historically known. Anthropology, mythology, demography, are bewilderingly manifold in their human material, whatever primordial images of recurrent patterns they discern within it. The contemporary difference is that the pluralisms are conscious. We live, to a degree hitherto unknown, in a period of universal history—thanks to speed, mobility, computering, and ubiquitous technology. We have multinational corporations and multinational corruption. Cultures interpenetrate and are more aware of doing so than

earlier generations knew, with their geographical isolations
and their spiritual *incommunicado.*

To be sure, there have been plenty of bold spirits who,
whether in trade or travel, pilgrimage or the pursuit of
learning, or utter wander-lust, drew strange experience from
strange lands. Al-Biruni, the celebrated scholar-traveller in
eleventh-century Islam, came to know Hinduism and India
with a wise discernment and a patient care. There were Jesuit
priests holding discourse in the court of the Mughal Emperor
Akbar in seventeenth-century Delhi. Martin Luther fostered a
translation of the Qur'an. It is well not to be too
congratulatory of ecumenism in decades recently passed, as if
only now Daniels were come to judgement. Frederick Denison
Maurice in the mid-nineteenth century was lecturing to good
effect on the religions of the world. Dialogue is no late idea.

Yet, wise as these reminders are, it is clear that there is a
religious feel for diversity which is new in its range and
alertness. Religious authority loses something of its identifying
and possessive character. Minorities are more ambitious to
survive   and   to   assert   themselves.   Eastern   presences
communicate within western society: western assumptions
permeate deeply into eastern living. In many of the issues of
thought and action the hemisphere is irrelevant to the question.
Religious factors, it is true, cannot be equated glibly. Indian
agriculture, for example, labours under the susceptibilities of
Hindus in ways that would never arise for the Marxist or for
Jewry in Israel. The effect, nevertheless, of common
denominators, such as the internationalism of science,
technological attitudes, the cult of efficiency, as well as sheer
material urgency, is to subdue, or at least diminish, the ability
of religious traditions to maintain their old monopolistic
dominance of culture.

This opening out of long seclusions of belief and mentality
tends   towards   another   significant   change.   Religious
optionality—if we may so term it—is increased for the person
by the weakening of static, communal assumptions of religious
identity. Birth still pre-determines religion for great masses of
humanity. But there is an evident trend away from such
inevitability towards some fluidity in faith participation. Even

strongly authoritarian systems are liable to leave more than they formerly did to individual conscience, partly, no doubt, as a wise tactic in the revision of rigorism.

This is not to say that we should anticipate, still less desire, a sort of buyer's market in religion. That notion misreads the nature of faith and its necessary context of nurture. Persons and beliefs cannot well be related as are merchants and merchandise.[6] Yet in Africa and Asia there is emerging, as there emerged much earlier in the west, a spirit of option, various as the factors are, in religious commitment. This is simply the pluralism reaching to the individual and its influence bears strongly, in subtle ways, even on those who have no mind for it.

Another feature deepening the Christian's sense of pluralism is the retrospect of two centuries of modern mission. From Carey to our own time most Christians have thought of the world's religions as territories for evangelism and longed for their response, in terms of conversion and baptism. But that long, devoted and sometimes heroic offer of the Gospel avails also to demonstrate the resilience and staying-power of ancient faiths in Asia. Though by no means impervious to Christian ministrations, they have, nevertheless, absorbed them in ways, for the most part, other than surrender to Christ. They have shown a power of survival and renewal in a period of external Christian opportunity, measured, sometimes dubiously, in terms of western rule, medical and educational philanthropy, and a long start in coping with modernity. Yet, despite such political subordination, social lethargy or intellectual stagnation, they have come through to recovery and self-revision. Primal patterns of culture, too, in Africa and the south seas, though more deeply permeable by Christian faith, have retrieved something of their cultural idiom from the late disruptions of their history.

The Christian, then, has to take the sobering fact that Asian religions have not yielded to mission in the form that missions assumed. The size of mission has grown in the pursuing of it. The penetrability of the physical world to travel is one thing, that of spiritual sanctuaries another. The ardour which, in the twenties of this century, could intend 'the evangelisation of the world in this generation', has a longer, soberer prospect in the seventies. What this means for the theology of mission we have to decide. The Christian who understands Christ will never be out of debt to the world, nor wanting in the will and the way to discharge it. Meanwhile, of course, the populations multiply. Buddhists, Hindus, Muslims, are far more numerous in the world than when modern mission began. Their nation-states bear an ever-enlarging responsibility for human well-being and the pursuit of peace. Pluralism, therefore, is not simply a fact of life but the condition and context of a Christian relevance in the world.

Our third prefatory reflection has to do with the pre-occupation in these times with the inner psyche. It might be said, not too extravagantly, that psychology is the 'pool of Bethesda' of our day. The characteristic eastern concern, which we will explore more fully in Chapter 3, is away from the questing, exploiting, mastering, intellectualist orientation of the classic western tradition, 'possessing the earth', and towards the solution of the inner mystery of the self. This direction away from rational aspiration, and into interior reading of the supposed clues of the psyche, the west has borrowed. But, unable to subdue the instincts of its scientism, it has been tempted to turn the eastern religious accounts of the self into a technique. Spirituality then ceases to be the quest for significance and becomes the cult of composure or the science of adjusted personality.

The consequences for the role of religion in life are very far-reaching. Meaning itself tends to be reduced to an analysable condition rather than received as an authentic possession. Values, their realising and cherishing, are then liable to be abandoned or suspected. Such suspicion, if pursued outwardly, recoils inwardly and becomes an inhibiting element in the very core of the self. When that happens, and deteriorates, we have the familiar drop-out situation which sociologists discuss and literature portrays. The frustrated self, finding only plausibility in society, opts out of its seeming pointlessness. Its sad conclusion is, in the words of Eugene Ionesco, that 'our culture no longer contains ourselves'.[7]

But that verdict, intended, it would seem, about a

society repudiated, has a double import. It also speaks of a self repudiating. 'Our culture no longer contains ourselves.' We are no longer really there, not merely in the sense that we feel it has no room in itself for us, but because we have no room in ourselves for it. In this withholding of ourselves from it, we forfeit ourselves within it. Whatever the outward factors, we owe ourselves to life and lose ourselves if we withdraw. Justifiable as our distrust of things, even our nausea, may be, the self cannot expect to be achieved in those terms, since to be is to meet. We must somehow accept the significance *of* ourselves if we are to find, and fulfil, it *in* ourselves.

In this necessity, it is futile to substitute a fascination with the mechanisms of the self, as much psychologism does, for the self in being. To take reality as that by which, in all likelihood, we are being cheated is to fail to take our very selfhood authentically.

Such 'loss of the self' in the very fabric of existence is a frequent feature in the art and writing of our day. Religion, in its deepest implications, is then most vitally at stake. For religion, in many of its manifestations, is the acceptance—grateful, resolute, timid, careful, reverent, puzzled, as the case may be—of the will to be. Even Asian faiths, with their doctrines of the flux of unreality, from which, as from illusion, the self must pass, may be seen as within such acceptance. Buddhist *samsara*, or stream of impermanence, requires a life-thesis, a goal, with the interim obligation of compassion. Its end in *nirvana* is not an interpretative indecision, a forfeiture, but a climax. Western, secular 'loss of the self', though sometimes loosely seen as akin and often recruiting yogic techniques, is something else. It has an ultimate neutralism within it. It lacks, as it were, the courage of its own distress.

For all their service to an understanding of ourselves, western sociology and psychology have followed the temptation of most sciences to enlarge unduly the area of their relevance and to subdue too much, as to meaning, to too little, as to category. When all their proper exploration of the workings, social and psychic, of the human situation, corporate and personal, is recognised, there remains the human reality, more than, larger than, their scrutinies as sciences. This more final significance, in and by all else, is that in the acceptance of which, however falteringly, religion lives.

As such, it has a debt of honesty to all that the sciences explore. To learn, for example, more deeply the intricacies of the psyche is to be denied easy religious illusions of innocence or of salvation. But it is to be left, nevertheless, in positive obligation to selfhood as to the real—the real as that which invites and deserves, not suspicion, but response. This means that we are summoned to deny the illusion that our being is inherently problematical and embrace instead the conviction that it is dependably significant. It is only fair to add that some of the most telling western writers in the communication of the lost self are among those who most clearly imply that the search for it persists. Nihilistic studies conclude the impossibility of nihilism. Despite frequent decisions and intentions to quit waiting, the final rubric of Samuel Beckett's *Waiting for Godot* is: 'They do not move.'[8] For, as Albert Camus has it: 'A literature of despair is a contradiction in terms.'[9] As long as the utter loss of significance generates a writing that finds it hauntingly significant then significance is restored. We are back, however paradoxically, with mystery and meaning, and with the self, however desperately, greeting them. We are back with religion.

This realisation brings us to the fourth main theme of reflection in this chapter, namely the recession of religious assurance. The paradox we have just reached remains for the most part undetected. The actual erosion of belief and practice is everywhere apparent. The factors inducing it are operative even where the outcome is delayed. Some have numbered the days of faith and announced them few.[10] Secularism, for many, seems the inescapable theme of the future.

With some the weakening of religious ties is an intellectual matter. Forms of doctrine seem outmoded in the changes of culture or fail to maintain their relevance in the flux of language. The committed mind of belief is held to be incompatible with the open mind of rational inquiry. Religions are compromised by obscurantism or stunted by rigorism. With others pluralism itself makes for scepticism or indifference. With religions comparative, one becomes comparatively religious. Decisive faith appears unnecessary or intolerant.

Or, for others again, the profession of sincere faith seems no longer viable in the actual world of competition and contention.

The madness of the times lies precisely in the existence, side by side, of a large number of unreconciled beliefs and attitudes ... the loudly proclaimed striving of all sections for the general interest when in fact each is pursuing very narrow and selfish particular ends. On each page of his newspaper the man in the street is confronted with a different and contradictory pattern of values. . . .

The challenge to make sense out of what appears as a senseless and fragmented action, the recognition that the fact that the modern world has lost its unifying principle is the source of its bewildering and soul destroying quality. . . .[11]

—these are likely to make us 'yield up all moral questions in despair', rather than aspire to sort them out, still less to link them to transcendent will and truth.

Others again are immersed in practical affairs, their energies, not least in Africa and Asia, harnessed to the claims of politics or development that leave no leisure for the luxury of the spiritual.

Whatever the reasons—these and others—they need to be closely in mind in the meeting of religions. There is the temptation to sharpen differences while bidding for declining interest. There is a tendency among them to suggest defensive alliances against materialism as a common enemy, or, yet again, to claim monopoly of competence against the foe. The issues deserve more perceptive and patient attitudes than these.

Some, of course, take refuge in renewed emphasis on certainty and truth within themselves. A world that is not persuaded needs to be more powerfully exhorted, more insistently addressed. Others, mostly in Christian quarters, have contrived to see almost a blessing in their experience of unwantedness.

God would have us know that we must live as men who
manage their lives without him. The God who is with us is
the God who forsakes us (Mark 15.34). The God who lets us
live in the world without the working hypothesis of God is
the God before whom we stand continually. Before God and
with God we live without God.[12]

But this is to confuse the autonomy which man biblically has
always possessed (it is no new discovery) with the neglect or
denial of the God-relatedness to which that autonomy was
always linked. Of course, the husbandmen are left with the
vineyard, but not without the Lord's relationship of trust and
expectation. Bonhoeffer only compounds the confusion when
he identifies the human autonomy under God with the enmity
that shapes the Cross of Jesus in the human world. For that
Cross is the supreme index of the meaning of his presence, not
'edged out' from, but Messianically within, our history.

   There were immediate circumstances of Bonhoeffer's
thinking which explain his words. But no careful Christian
perspective can ever make a virtue of secularity. The human
autonomy which allows of it, only does so as rejection of the
proper calling into consecration. Sacredness, for us, does not
stand in some reservation of nature from our hands and from
our sciences. On the contrary, it means the hallowing which is
due from our reverent possession. In so far as secularity is the
will to deny such hallowing it can never be intelligently
applauded by those who understand whom they have believed
in the creation and the Cross. For the rest, the secular, with
discernment, may be our ally. To aspects of this discernment
we may return in Chapter 6.

   Other faiths have interesting reactions to those Christians
who find in secularism the human destiny to get along without
God and the divine will to be humanly negligible. Writers in
Judaism comment with a wry smile that Christians are at last
discovering how costly and paradoxical it is to be 'a chosen
people'. Jews have long ago learned to live in the seeming
absence of divine concern. To Muslims secularism, they claim,
is never a problem, past or future, since Islam has always
identified faith and society, belief and the state. As for

Buddhists, the whole question stems directly from the illusoriness of existence and from the false thesis of a creative will where there is only karmic necessity.

But, however religions decide about irreligion, what, in the fifth place, we have called the argument between change and hope will always obtain. The point to realise in all that follows is that religions themselves are not static. Traditionalism and perpetuation are doubtless dear to them, as to all venerable things in history. But change is perpetual also and never more evident among them than today. It would be wrong to imagine any of the great faiths as fixed, or to relate to them with set notions of their character, however verified by historians those notions might seem. Indeed, the historians themselves are involved in the issues about identity and content. Argument reaches back into the reading of the past, the interpretation of sacred scriptures and the nature of loyalty to institutions. The present, when it wants the past on its side, is liable to re-write it. The documents, too, may undergo, as it were, a revision of intent. The Gita, in the experience of Gandhi, is not the Gita of its first contemporaries. Moses to Martin Buber has a different significance from that which he had to the defenders of Masada. How should we relate the Jesus of Emerson to the Christ of Calvin?[13]

This need not mean any sort of despair. Change is not total: it remains an argument. Disparity is within identity. Plainly, if change were thought to be total, there would be no entity in which it could be registered. Buddhism, Hinduism, Judaism, Islam, the primal religions, are recognisably themselves but only in the flow of time and transition. We have Neo-Buddhism, Neo-Hinduism: Islam, in Muhammad Iqbāl's phrase, with 'a reconstruction of [its] religious thought'.[14] Moreover, there has been a large degree of interaction between particular faiths in the long contacts of their history in shared territories and mingling populations or circumstances of mutual political and cultural exposure.

Much responsibility between religions today has to do with this flux within them all. We need to beware that we are not relating unawares to what is already disengaging with itself. Even immigrant communities, in their defensiveness, may not be conscious of what is transpiring among their co-religionaries in the lands of dominance. To understand the often common constraints in changing times, and to care for the directions taken, may be the cue to more ultimate relationships and ministries of mind.

The argument of change with hope, going on under the pressures of the contemporary scene and of the inner momentum of the past, belongs, of course, to the elemental fact of the sequence of generations. At the outset of this chapter, we noted the Qur'an's repeated interest in man the procreator, the procreated. 'Let Thy work appear unto Thy servants and Thy glory unto their children', sang the psalmist (90.16). It is this flux of the generations which forbids the hardening of the inflexible. For it entails a continual transmission of the custody of faith. It means initiation by legacy, an unceasing passage of nurture beyond the nurtured. Survival is only by renewal. Since custodians pass, custody may alter. As long as the human is perennially relinquished in the aged and begun anew in the youthful, faith, too, and religion as its expression, will, likewise, be involved with hope. What we are studying, then, in these chapters, is not so much a closed pool of reflection as the retreating wake behind a moving thing.

This means no easy optimism. 'Coming of age', mused Pip in *Great Expectations*, 'seemed hardly worth while at all in such a guarded and suspicious world as Jaggers had made of it.'[15] Youth has no guarantees in a sombre time. Expectations, nevertheless.

'This Earth, my Brother.' Man is fellow to man in the same world, a world where, more than before, he is *neah-gebur*, neighbour, nigh and boor, near and an earth-dweller, a peasant, a rustic—the oldest of technicians. Meeting, encounter, whatever it is we intend, begins from that 'neighbourhood' of men.

2 The right courtesies

'THESE people's politeness really set us up again in our own esteem. We had a thirst for consideration, the sense of insult was still hot on our spirits: and the civil usage seemed to restore us to our position in the world.' In *An Inland Voyage* Robert Louis Stevenson recovers from a bruising surliness elsewhere in the civilities that met him in La Fère. Adjacent villages in the same river basin could be quite contrasted in their reception. Such human 'thirst for consideration' is everywhere to be found. It is well for any study of Christian relationships with other men in their faiths to begin in the same praise of courtesy. As a faith whose heart conviction has to do with the hospitality of God in the human world, Christianity is surely bound to practise it towards the other guests, the more so if they have yet to know themselves in that capacity.

This is not to argue some sentimental complaisance. Nor is it to miss the strenuous things. These we have to come to in the sequel. But, necessary to any hope for them, is this prerequisite of spiritual courtesy. If a 'sense of insult still hot upon our spirits' is too sharp a phrase to fit all present attitudes in Africa and Asia, it certainly describes the sense of injury and exploitation that other cultures feel. Contemporary history pictures many gestures of rejection or of self-sufficiency. The susceptibilities of the quarter-century or so of post-imperial developments, through which we have just passed, persist beyond the political events which were supposed to satisfy them.

Courtesy, however, is the proper temper not only because it helps restore people to themselves, countering resentments and suspicions. It is, further, the only right mentality with religious truth. An anxious apologist is, clearly, a contradiction in

17

terms. If his confidence in truth needs to be bolstered by arrogance it shows itself misplaced. Witness and incivility cannot well combine. Often ill-served as they are, there is about the themes of religions a fundamental awe and ultimacy fit to silence clamour and shame mere competition. The Buddhist 'reverence for reverence' is appropriate to all in this context, differ as the logic will by which it may be reached. There is a sense in which churlishness to another's religion is like discourtesy in his dwelling, or hostility at his table. For, in the deepest reaches, faith is where the human is at once most vulnerable and most intimate.

Or, if not from seemliness in guests, we might draw a parallel from a quality in artists, at least those in the temper of a seventeenth-century Chinese manual of painting.

> When you paint a man looking at a mountain, the man should be slightly bent in appropriate homage to so lordly a being: and the mountain, too, should seem to be bowing slightly and with permissive dignity towards the man. In the same way when a lutist is playing out music from his lute under the moon, he should seem to be listening to the moon, and the moon in turn . . . should appear to be listening to the lute player.[1]

In so far as the student of religion resembles a painter, he may well make his pictures truer for a like sense of deference within them.

Other chapters must probe this further, but, as a point of departure, and as a steady set of mind, it is a proper plea. The necessities of controversy belong within the habits of respect. To treat religious experience is to move amid the sacred, however we may want to think it misconstrued. It is to walk amid the dreams of men, to see into the farthest reaches of their confidence and their dismay, to overhear them in their ultimate decisions. There is no place here for insensitive behaviour.

The purpose of this chapter is to consider aspects of the meaning of such courtesy, as the expression of an inward integrity and the condition of a right outward meeting. Courtesy intends a truth of relationship as the necessary prelude to truth in communication. Faith, wisely understood, is not an option of assents transferable by propositions. Rather, it is a pattern of response to meaning that is realised. Reflection makes it clear that much controversy arises from resentment. Beliefs are identified with enmities, or, if not identified, then certainly entangled. Unless the enmities are surmounted, the beliefs remain either suspect or obscure. Then argument becomes the dominant idea and vindication becomes paramount. Then reasons are overtaken by motives or turn into them. However well- or ill-disguised as logical, counsel is darkened by partisan emotion. The very nature of relevance is then distorted and can only be restored if there is a deliberate recognition of how far prejudice has supervened. If new hope is to come to birth in such a situation, courtesy is surely its most likely midwife.

The issue of the caste system in India is notoriously controversial. The relation between caste and Hinduism is so complex. Aspects of the system—untouchability, apathy, determinism—are so easily castigated and reproached by the outsider. But he may well miss the intricacies of what he instinctively condemns, knowing, perhaps, little or nothing of the original theory of a fourfold division of the human life-span, from birth to death, nor yet of the social implications of fulfilling an accepted role, nor yet again of the karmic view for which being never *is* but only evermore becoming. Unmindful of these, and of the tensions here of Hinduism within itself, the critic, in his condemnation, may provoke only irritation. The Hindu reaction reaches out for alibis, for *tu quoque* defences. What sadly needs a common and incisive care recedes into obfuscating contention.

Thus, for example, Dr I. C. Sharma in *Ethical Philosophies of India*, expounds the Upanishadic sources of the original 'ethico-social organization of the Hindus' which 'aimed at the all-round development of the personality of the individual and the wellbeing of society'. But he goes on to link the conventional caste system with political vicissitudes. 'The synthetic view', the truly Hindu one, was lost to sight because of 'foreign domination thwarting' Indian culture, dooming Hinduism to stultifying traditions, for lack of 'research in Indology', until the British Raj culminates and completes the process, its only blessing being the disguised one by which it provokes an ultimate reaction and Indology comes to its own rescue.[2] Such pleading is understandably predictable, likely enough considering all the intellectual problems of Indo-western relationships, but, for all that, hardly convincing as it stands. All faiths and cultures are liable to just such arts of self-assessment. The question must be whether such diversionary thinking could perhaps be retrieved for surer diagnosis by a better quality of courtesy in the first place. The Bhagavad Gita deserves better than to be discounted by a tourist's repulsion amid the sights of Benares, just as Hinduism is capable of a fuller obligation to its observers than referring them to the burden of the British presence. But such deeper reaches of relationship, either to other, can only be attained by going mutually beyond superficial verdicts and equally incomplete responses. Courtesy as a steady purpose might best foster such an end.

Much Buddhist thinking—to turn elsewhere—has registered its feeling of injustice at some forms of Christian rejection. Its *Nirvana*, it is said, is annihilation, a negation of all meaning in an ultimate denial of the very self of man. The Christian preciousness of personality—as we shall see elsewhere—has reason to be scandalised. For the implications are radical. But it is well to get the matter straight. Only a careful deference to truth will do so. One cannot truly say that 'The self is annihilated', inasmuch as a self to annihilate does not really exist. The act of deploring such a negative concept of salvation itself turns on misapprehending it. Annihilation, in one sense, is true enough, but only in that the illusion by which identity clings to isolatedness is terminated. One needs Christian beliefs about creaturehood and creation, about history and the self, to have need to resist the denial of them. Buddhism, however, does not hold these beliefs, nor their criteria of how we should understand the world. Accordingly, it is not judged by the supposition of them, since the supposition itself is excluded.

What is at stake here needs urgently to be explored, but only after first acknowledging where the exploration takes us. The Buddhist doctrine of *anatta*, or not-self, does not say, for example: 'Here I am, being angry; I must put such anger from me, calm myself and be anger-free.' That way, there will still be me purposefully dealing with my anger and very much present in 'my' victory over it. Rather a state must be sought where *sunyata*, or emptiness of self, is attained where, effectively, there is non-anger, but not as a conscious thrust negating, and so still preoccupied with, its presence. Meditative disciplines are the road to this goal.

The instinctive Christian feeling here that one has been subjected to some sleight of hand, some verbal subtlety, is clear and strong. It is likely to grow more so when one hears it said: 'If any one says that the *Tathagata* sets forth a Teaching, he really slanders the Buddha and is unable to explain what I teach. As to any truth-declaring system, Truth is undeclarable.'[3] For that sounds deliberately elusive and seems negligent of the law of contradiction. The Christian is naturally uneasy, accustomed as he is to believing his beliefs, if he hears himself being told that such very understanding is not to be so understood. He does not take readily to embracing a cloud. For this is a skill he has not been trained to practise.

Only an instinctive courtesy can save him here from precipitate judgements where rich issues will be impatiently foreclosed. He must beware the instinct to set simplicity (his) over against evasion (theirs). Those tables can so easily be turned and the roles reversed. Moreover, as in all these encounters of faiths, there is inwardness only on opposite sides. Each party knows his own familiar world from behind its own windows, the other knows it, if at all, only by looking in from outside. The glass turns back his penetration or yields deceptive impressions. This situation is reciprocal. This externality of the other to me could, indeed, be in itself sufficient ground for the whole plea that asks 'reverence for reverence'. For only so is there hope that first impressions will not also be final.

There is interesting corroboration of this ready to hand from quite a different quarter, namely Martin Buber's classic discussion of Jewish/Christian faith in *Two Types of Faith*. It is sad to register how so acute and sympathetic a mind could have so far formalised the comparison and missed the measure of actual community that exists between the characterisations his exposition contrasts. As in many other cases of such comparison, including those which Christians make, it is the domestic which emerges favourably, the foreign otherwise. There have been many Christian presentations 'inferiorising' (if we may mint the word) the contents of Judaism.

Buber—and this is perhaps significant for our warning—imprisons himself at the outset within two items of vocabulary, namely *pistis* and *emunah*. Terms, of course, are vital for thought. But they only take life in persons. *Pistis*, conceptual faith, he says, is what Christians have: *emunah*, existence in fidelity, is Judaic. The former is believing *that* . . ., the latter trusting *in* and belonging *with*. The distinction can then be drawn in parallel lines of explicit contrast with little doubt, for the reader, where the evident preference must lie. *Pistis* is propositional: it acknowledges as true the facts it credits: by acceptance man enters into identity, 'facing about', as Buber puts it, in purely individual terms. Such faith is likely to be argumentative and, by implication, acquired and formal, making for an orthodoxy. *Emunah*, on the other hand, means trusting a person, counting on relationship, taking the divine as real within the already constituted reality of nationhood. The *emunah*-style 'believer' finds himself 'persisting in covenant', having a position in truth, rather than holding a doctrine of truth.

How strange that a mind so perceptive and irenic should have presented so doctrinaire a scheme by which to relate two deeply wrought religions, where so many features cry out against generalisations. Is there not a degree of believing *that* in any possibility of trusting *in*? Need the community in truth confessed, which Christianity discovers, be altogether contrasted with community in covenant which Judaism believes? Is there not a founding element in Christian experience, unbroken from Paul to Hammarskjöld, *via* Francis, Luther and Kierkegaard, which would at least qualify, as Buber himself, happily, seems aware, the idea that Christians live simply by propositions to which they give their credence? For these, discipleship stood in terms of faithfulness, received and given, 'in Christ'. Can the truest Judaic reliance on covenantal experience elude the formulation, in some measure, of chosenness, covenant and destiny, as items of belief not improperly to be affirmed?[4]

So puzzling from one angle is the seeming partisanship of mind here, that we have to search for an explanation in the psyche—which, of course, is where we find it. Jewish experience in the Christian context has been harsh. Its deepest inward burden, in Buber's own phrase, is 'the unredeemedness of the world'.[5] In face of the world as history shows it to be, how can Christians say that 'the world is redeemed', that Messiahship has happened in Jesus. Aside from the ancient question whether suffering can properly be his credential, Messiah never comes historically. To *have* him is no longer to await him or to seek him. So the Christian must be the incurable romantic, the inveterate believer *that* . . .,[6] the man with the proposition which, since experience disallows it, dogma must the more abstractedly assert it. Meanwhile the Judaic continues in a proper style of being, cast upon a divine fidelity which it refuses to tie down to historical particulars, the more so since those historical particulars have so grievously burdened one's own history in the manner of their affirmation. There is a deep sense in which, for a Jew, to credit Christian *pistis* is to forsake a Judaic *emunah*. So loyalty to loyalty abides. But the essential rejection is in the psyche: it is 'the reasons of the heart' which decide the logic of *Two Types of Faith* and, so deciding, miss 'the reasons of the other's heart.'

Much else, abridged in this summary, belongs with the *pistis/emunah* question. For our present purpose, it is easy to see, yet again, how a potentially alienating line-up of ideas has to be handled patiently. Only a resolute courtesy can begin to do so. Then, perhaps, we can begin to say that a Messiahship we *can* identify within history does not mean an idle romanticism which merely believes *that* it is so. On the contrary, it is of a sort—as we shall see later—as to recruit and require us in its *present* tense of action. The redeemed must be the redeeming: to believe ourselves met Messianically, by 'God in Christ', is to be called into fidelity to the principle of the Cross always. This is not a *pistis* which excludes or dispenses with *emunah*. Rather it generates, educates and

sustains it. The Christian has to take the point while reversing
the conclusion. What could be further from the meaning of the
Cross than to think it understood as an exoneration from any
liability except credence, or as an invitation to complacence?
Given courtesy of mind, however, it is the very length of the
misconceptions which give us pause about ourselves. The
business of any intelligent faith is to care for the image it
presents in the glass of others' vision. 'Meaning *of* . . .' can
never be divorced from 'meaning *for* . . .' Since meaning is a
transaction with others, and not a commodity, as it were, in
stock, relationship is inseparable from faith, and faith from
relationship.

These ready, if random, examples could well be multiplied.
Similar issues will arise below in other contexts. All we are
here concerned to do is to argue courtesy as a first requisite of
truth and the trust of it in expression. It is well to reflect on this
a little further, since doctrine is usually thought of as vital to
Christian relationships and emphasis on it the first, if not the
sole, element in our Christian loyalty both to Christ and
people. 'If the trumpet give an uncertain sound . . .' tends to be
promptly invoked by many wherever there is suspicion that the
trumpet sounds uncertainly. 'We are bound in so far to
dogmatise because it concerns man's salvation that we
should',[7] wrote Austin Farrer, for 'theology is a life and death
concern'.

We will see from another angle in the next chapter the force
of this view. It is historically characteristic of Christian, and
indeed of Muslim, attitudes. Clarity and authority, aiding each
other, are likely to be the more prized *vis-à-vis* those Asian
religions which often seem to discount them. But
understandable as these feelings are, it should be clear that
they do not tell the whole story. Much of the tradition of
dogma derives from internal, domestic tensions within a faith's
history, from the need to exclude and identify heresy. That
consideration, in its due limits, is not appropriate to the
definition of faith-relationships beyond domestic frontiers. The
definition of what is *de fide* for the *fideles* is one thing: trust of
truth on behalf of other religions is another. Religions have an
identity, a momentum, an ethos of their own and, within the

plural world, are not subject to the intellectual criteria or the spiritual credentials of their neighbours—not, at least, until we have together explored those criteria and credentials as far as we may within some agreed reference-frame of human experience. To accost the other believer with the interior preconditions of dogma would be to foreclose, perhaps prejudice, such exploration. Authority can hardly be arbitrary and be also 'religious': to assert it as the adequate ground of its own right to adjudicate is to assume as finished a task which is not begun. Yet too often it is taken for granted that the proper exercise of religious authority over the limits, and content, of what is faith for the faithful extends indifferently to its encounter with other faith-systems. The great faith-systems are far from being heresies of ours. Nor are their adherents explicitly liable to our constraints; in the world we are not, so to speak, applying an 'orthodoxy'. We are living with *polydoxia.*

To take this position is not to impugn the authority of revelation on its own ground. We are right to affirm to the world: 'God has spoken to us in His Son', and to mean by 'us' the whole community of mankind. Indeed, we do not confess our faith if we privatise its reach. While *our* sense of conviction, in so affirming, and the status both of the conviction and of the Scriptures in which, dependably, it is housed for us, are important elements in its truth-claim, they cannot well be the arbitrary ground of their warrant to a hearing. 'Thus saith the Lord' is a claim which stands, not in its vehemence but its audibility.

The interreligious situation of Christian doctrine suggests another consideration. Even internally to our Christianity, dogma, often thought of as defensive, preservative, even clinical, ensuring truth, must be seen also as hospitable and inviting. Frontiers that need guards and guardians also enclose areas in which liberties are secured. Faith, as credally defined, is a territory to inhabit, a house to occupy, as well as a fence to maintain and a wall to build. What matters is that habitation should be open to prospectives as well as defensible to inhabitants. Doctrine means invitation to discovery as well as warning against deviation, and for the same reason. This role needs to be steadily kept in view. 'Uncertain sounds' may come equally from loud tones as from gentle ones. We are sometimes most forthright when we are least convincing.

The deep sense the Christian must surely feel, namely that he is in trust with truth he has no mandate to barter but only to serve and to share, must always be paramount. The question about witness is not Whether? but How? There must be no evasion of issues, as we will maintain below. But they must be appropriately joined. This means that they must be allowed to emerge *within*, rather than merely against, the intimate meanings and preoccupations of the other man's world. An alert sense of the relevance to us and to our witness, of what otherwise we might be minded to dismiss or to dispute, is truly consistent with the positive and inward loyalties of Christian doctrine.

This practice of deference, if we may so speak, in the Christian temper in the multireligious setting, may be illustrated in a different context. A cultural parable may be found useful, both for what it illuminates and for the sense in which it falls short.

Leopold Sedar Senghor, President of Senegal, is well-known for his concept of *négritude*, or the sense of being Negro, with a wealth of arts, culture, history and proper ethnic pride. He has made this concept the central factor in his leadership. 'Seek ye first the cultural kingdom and all else will be added . . . ' is the way, if at all, he would paraphrase the Sermon on the Mount.[8] The clue to the commerce of cultures and races lies in each being self-possessed in dignity and free in spirit. Hence his steady urge to express black African experience and creativity.

But to others the programme of *négritude* seemed apologetic and naïve, as if saying, lamely: 'Alright, you despise me: let me show you, however, that I don't deserve to be. I have this and this in my history. I have much to glory in: you needn't think I feel ashamed.' Such pleading seemed, to minds like Frantz Fanon, a still unliberated, colonialised mind, evading the necessary passionate de-colonialising of its thinking. Its very pride was craven-hearted: its self-assertion still intimidated, mild-minded, looking for compensation, admiring wattle huts when it should be clutching grenades. Wole Soyinka, in

Nigeria, asked pointedly whether a tiger need proclaim his *tigritude*? Fanon denounced it furiously in *The Wretched of the Earth.* To rehabilitate nativeness, for these writers, seemed to concede that it had been properly disparaged. Fanon, at least, demanded a wholly militant relationship. His consequent appeal to violence required him to embrace all in a stereotype. Culture itself was only valid in revolution: hearts were only pure when hands were bloody. *Négritude* had to be anathema, because Frenchmen had to be. One could not gain one's world without denunciation.

Yet it is notable that Senghor achieved a far more penetrating awareness of western culture and an infinitely more relaxed and positive humanism than the tortured mind of Fanon's heroics.

It is not that Senghor is lacking in the will to indict imperialism or to accuse the west.

Fanon did not want the white man to *grant* the black man anything. By contrast, Senghor, allowing himself to withdraw into what cynics called 'the twilight past of African culture', found a spiritual liberty to affirm the primacy of the spiritual in all men. He was free to offer because he was free to receive. Western spirituality did not have to be repudiated in order that his Serer society could be self-possessed. Nor did his own identity have to be compromised in being open to humanity. Senghor had the breadth of spirit in which relationships did not have to be brutalised or polemicised. The leisure to be open was one with the will to participate.

It was so, to be sure, more by African and Christian spontaneity, than by any western deserts. But, nevertheless, the pattern illustrates the courtesy spirit, giving and receiving, even against all the odds of history. In so far as religions are cultures—which is a considerable way—with legacies of pride and tradition, the lesson is clear. It is when they are allowed their cultural selves that they can best reach beyond themselves. It is when they are consciously under threat that they are suspiciously isolated in temper. It is only when we are allowed our own humanity that we seek an inclusive humanness. Reciprocal courtesy is, therefore, the wisest, as well as the truest, prescript for relationship.

But there is a point where this proper parable halts. Historical religions are cultural identities. But they are more. The cultural does not exhaust their significance. It cannot, therefore, determine their whole duty to each other. Each with a wide diversity of cultural expression, they have to do with the nature and meaning of the human beneath the fashion of time, the form of symbol, the pattern of myth and ritual, the themes of art, within which, as religions, they proceed. They claim, under these bearers of their meaning, to interpret and guide the human condition. In variant ways, they purport to identify the real and to serve the eternal, to feel with the transcendent or to love the divine. It is part of this will to 'truth' that it accept its own inclusiveness, its liability, that is, to belong with all its dimensions. They cannot, then, halt at mutual, cultural respect. Their courtesies, in that sense, must be responsible for a deeper seriousness than mere co-existence. Each ought to take account of the others' verdicts, whether kindred or alien, neighbourly or distant. Relevance *in* any religion is relevance *for* all. While they may be deliberately separate in their findings, they are common in their human habitation. Perhaps the largest test of their integrity is their integrity about each other. The courtesy which should guide their temper cannot, of itself, decide their agenda.

Before turning to that task, there is one final consideration proper to this chapter. The concern, in all that follows, is broadly with religions in their world setting, in their politico-cultural 'establishments' in co-existence today, rather than with the special problems of minority communities, whether, for example, Copts in Egypt, or Muslims in Britain, or Hindus in Sri Lanka. Yet the behaviour of faiths in circumstances of majority privilege towards others in minority status is a sensitive part of the entire question. Minorities, too, though this is less readily acknowledged, have duties to majority culture. But it is primarily with majorities that the obligations lie. Clearly, courtesy is here the more manifestly proper, where situations hold many temptations to pressure on the one hand and to suspicion on the other.

The minority, even if in freely chosen exile from its majority world, senses insecurity, fears for survival, worries about compromise, is anxious for the next generation. Contact with the majority culture and its religious forms is likely to be apprehensive and psychologically disadvantageous, rather than relaxed and intelligent.

Here Jewish experience has been the most tragic and prolonged, unique in its intensity but one in kind with that of other displacements and diasporas down the centuries. As Zionist thinking came to formulate it, this last century, the host-nation situation (as the phrase has it) is such as to allow in the end only two alternatives, neither of them acceptable. There is either the ghetto, with persecution when hostility rules, or assimilation where tolerance obtains. But the latter, in a strange way, is no less inimical than the former. For it threatens the continuity of the faith by detaching, as it were, the faithful from their faith identity and, with the passage of time, approximating them into the dominant culture. Such toleration, it is held by Zionism, is a sort of conditional toleration. It acknowledges only on the implied condition of likely assimilation. It says, in effect, that the price of survival, albeit subtly exacted over the years, is surrender.[10] Hence the 'final' Zionist solution which, rejecting both the ghetto and assimilation, and with them the host-nations concept of dispersion altogether, determines to establish independent statehood as the one secure condition and guarantee of religious continuity.

It is that very logic, in a paradoxical way, which confirms the whole plea of this chapter. For diasporas do, and will, continue. There are no more Israels, no more Pakistans creatable to care, in national terms, for the security of Jews in the world, or for Muslims in the sub-continent. National havens may aspire to protect more than they enclose. But to see them as a *sine qua non* is a philosophy which despairs for any human tolerance of diversity of an ultimately dependable kind. Yet it relies on a solution which is by no means a universal option.

So it is that we need to learn a shape of recognition which leaves minorities, where there is no path to salvation by separate statehood, relaxed and secure. In some measure the growth of secularity may do this for us, though only as a by-product which diminishes at the same time the quality of the courtesy we owe. If host-nations there are bound to be, as long as time lasts, then the more important is it that their hospitality be right. But this takes us into reaches of the religious situation for which thus far we have only been preparing.

3   Dimensions of religion

'ALL music is what awakes from you when you are reminded by the instruments', wrote Walt Whitman in his famous *Leaves of Grass*. That certainly goes for dance and march and song, and perhaps for the symphony also. Religion, like music, is hard to define. Both live in the interplay of soul and significance, of reality akin and yet beyond ourselves, of meaning in its own right and of response in ours. Worship is just such an awakening to relationship amid reminders that surround us everywhere.

A well-known phrase in the New Testament puts this sense of things with telling simplicity. The writer in Heb. 4.13 speaks of God as 'Him with whom we have to do'. The 'we' here is Christian. The Greek verb in the verse might be literally translated: 'He to whom there is for us the word', or: 'He to whom the word is ours'. God, it says, is addressable, conversible. The 'having to do' of the familiar Authorised Version is a talking, a speaking, a relationship of prayer, a sense of being relevant, he to us and we to him. It is precisely that 'he' and 'us' which make the Christian situation. God is the theme of a human *logos* for the reason that God has a *logos*-relatedness to our humanity. Christianity, we may say, is God answering to his Name. That conviction stands at the opposite pole to the harsh and bitter comment: 'The only excuse for God is that He does not exist.' Heb. 4.13 uses the third person because it is describing an experience. When that experience is itself vocal 'Thou, Lord', and 'Our Father', are its pronouns.

But, Christian as the intention is, the phrase has clearly a rich inclusive ring. The writer stands in a long tradition of Judaic faith where 'heart and flesh cry out for the living God'.

31

'True prayer', it has been claimed, 'is the creation of the Jews.'[1]
In different idiom, but in no finally alien way, Islam also cries:
'Thee it is we worship, Thee it is to whom for aid we turn.' For
these, and potentially for all, God is the terminal point of all
our interrogation of life, all our wonder and puzzlement about
who, and why, we are—God the addressee of man.

Within the verse in Hebrews there is a vivid metaphor which
reads: 'All things are open and upturned before the eyes of
Him with whom we have to do.' To appreciate the second
adjective we need to imagine the opposite of the Rodin
sculpture used on the cover of Bishop John Robinson's *Honest
to God*. Instead of the burdened, musing, downcast figure, the
picture here is of a hand below the chin, lifting up the head of a
friend to interrogate the face. There is that which invites,
kindles and searches our response. What we do in our religion
is the answer of our souls to the reality of the divine concern.
Experience, as we know it humanly, is here understood as
anxiety, hope and mystery, living their aspiration and their
perplexity as proper to the heart of things. For all the radical
divergence this chapter must trace, it might be possible to
claim that here in this simple clause of Heb. 4.13, we have a
measure of religion from which we can begin. If only in
preliminary terms we may take man, thus vocal before God, to
represent what we may call the faiths of pronounal confidence,
of divine–human encounter, in the shape of theistic religion.
Their nature will be clearer when we come, below, to those
contrasted patterns which quite repudiate pronounal prayer
and the language of 'I' and 'Thou'. Christian distinctiveness
within the theisms will be reached in Chapter 4. Meanwhile,
the purpose is to explore the meaning of the 'word' we 'have' to
say to God and of the upturned face that speaks.

'Exploration' is, indeed, itself the first realm of the 'word'. 'O
that I knew where I might find Him', cried Job (Job 23.3).
'Verily, Thou art a God that hidest thyself', said the prophet
(Isa. 45.15). Faith might well be defined as what men do about
the strangeness of the world, their concern with the enigma of
their own being, and the sense that the clue is to be sought in
personal relationship as that into which the whole field of
common experience tends and points. In such will to discover,

to relate, to understand, to belong, the self is most fully alive, cognisant and true, as contrasted with the indifference, or the ennui, or the malaise which abandons the appetite for meaning and for truth.

Both solitariness and community pervade such exploration. 'There are many with me', as the psalmist realised (Ps. 55.18). For the yearning is perennial. Yet it is properly one's own, inalienable and inward. 'The sea is so wide and my boat is so small.' The quest is, at once, universal and private, everyman's and mine. Why? and whence? and whither? We wonder, and surmise, and dream, and speculate, and conjecture. We interrogate our own faculties of search, mind and reason, heart and feeling, will and purpose. The questions of knowledge involve what faculties we can trust, as well as what meanings we can affirm. They have to include the very assumption that the search is a search for God. For to take conjecture for conclusion is to disqualify the searching. Premature conviction, in a sense, is no conviction at all. The same has to be true of premature non-conviction, whether through spite, or weariness, or evasion, or confusion.

In either case, there *is* 'for us the word', a catechising of all our experience, within the onus of personal being. Faith, thus far, is no less than the will to refuse the unexamined life, to be open to the whole, to let the heart respond and the will care, to let life be the mystery it is—as only persons can. Such exploration reaches far deeper than the mere search for causalities within phenomena. There has really been no search if we think, in the odd contemporary way, that God, as they say, is elided, dead by a thousand qualifications, because we have found explanations for events which were formerly attributable to his 'direct action'. This is to imagine, obtusely, that God has gone with the going of a 'gap' where ignorance might locate him. What we have to wonder at is explicability itself, not this or that phenomenon for which explanation can be found in nature. Science, even when we suppose that its findings are final, still leaves us with the scientist, with man in his competence, restlessly pursuing rest. There are no gaps from which meaning can elide in the perpetual, human dimension of the arts and of the imagination. The exploration that can end in laboratories has scarcely begun.

That 'there is for us the word' means not only exploration but, shall we say, expectancy? The theisms, certainly, have this instinctive sense that the search might be reciprocated, that it would not be the thing it is if it were one-directional. For the prophet the very hiddenness of God was somehow also an invitation. Significance, indeed, is always relational. Perhaps man's very nature *qua* person stands in a homing instinct, in the sense of the opening of Ps. 90: 'O Lord, Thou hast been a home for us in all generations.' There could hardly be a wound of absence if there were no meaning to a presence. As we noted in Chapter 1, the very portrayal of nihilism suggests its impossibility.

This is not to claim that the hope of revelation allows us to assert the fact of it. But if we can have an honest hope about *whether* it might be, we can the more perceptively consider *where*. In daily experience there are certainly many spheres of an inward/outward relationship. To find the world, in the scientific sense, intelligible is to involve ourselves with intelligence, even if we forebear to personalise it divinely. To experience the world, in a poetic sense, as entrancing and inexhaustibly joyous is to feel that maybe there is an artist at the heart of it. To know the world, in a moral sense, as the steady scrutiny of our sincerity of will, is to conjecture that there is a purpose of persons in its very structure. Perhaps the implications of these features may be looked for further. If all things are, in some measure, revelatory of God, or truth, then perhaps particulars among them, or brought to pass within them, can be supremely revelatory. We need not suppose a central cluelessness in a world so full of clues.

Expectancy, then, is what anticipates that which revelation (i.e. historical, within general, revelation) is understood as bestowing. It is wise to keep the link close between the two. For a deep credential of historical revelation is precisely the conviction that it concerns, illuminates, in a way answers, the questions which experience presents. When the apostle, quoting Deuteronomy (Deut. 30.14), insists that 'the word is nigh thee' (Rom. 10.8), there is more than a good memory in mind. What is given in revelation coincides deeply with what is yearned for in the soul. When meaning glimpsed becomes meaning confirmed, experience and revelation may be said to complement each other.

This is not at all to say that wishfulness devises its own satisfaction. On the contrary, as we must see, there are profoundly disconcerting answers to our expectancy. Nor is it to miss the sense of overwhelming initiative from God in 'the word that is nigh'.[2] But that very initiative, to be apt for our receiving, cannot be arbitrary, a sort of celestial asserting unrelated to our receiving. Revelation, properly understood, is not communiqué but apprehension, and cannot ensue unless, like a bridge, it belongs with either side of what it spans.[3] For all its spontaneous grace, it is a speaking into our condition, a responsiveness to our expectancy. It is the upturning of our face.

'This is the Lord, we have waited for Him' (Isa. 25.9) is, in some sense, the language of revelatory religion. As the poet, the painter, the musician, find their kindred realms of meaning answering their souls, so faith reads its answering significance in the events, the words, the personalities within history which, enshrined in scriptures, spell truth. The confidence of the Old Testament gathers around Sinai and 'Thus saith the Lord'. 'In Jewry is God known' (Ps. 76.1). The eternal wisdom pitched his tent in Israel. History, as the purpose of creation, discloses the waywardness of man the creature and therefore calls aloud for the retrieving of the broken glory by means of the Messianic hope.

That hope the New Testament identifies in the figure of Jesus crucified. For the ministry of word and deed which is the prelude to those sufferings comes to its climax in an act of rejection and perversity in which we may discern, as in a single focus, all the waywardness that is Messiah's burden. The community of faith in the New Testament comes to birth in the dimensions of the answer of redeeming love with which that burden is assumed in suffering and death. Who Messiah is is known in how he is. The knowledge is transforming of the very hope that greets it and carries the Church into new discoveries of the nature of Messiah's God, now recognisable in this Christ, and of the nature of human community in which there is 'neither Jew nor Greek'. Expectancy is incredibly fulfilled and knows itself remade in the fulfilling. 'God has spoken to us in His Son' (Heb. 1.2). The conclusion is: 'The Word was made flesh and dwelt among us and we beheld His glory' (John 1.14). The initiative was God's, the recognition ours.

The Qur'an, the Islamic Scripture, might seem less readily fitted into this context of expectancy. For it possesses, in the Muslim temper, an almost entire emphasis on the divine will. But that, it may be claimed, is only a natural form of the desire for certainty, or for certification. The Qur'an is *given*, in a more absolute sense, as its faithful understand it, than any other Scripture. Yet it relates to what the Book itself calls *fitrat-Allah* (Surah 30.30), that human nature, or quality, in which God 'natured' mankind. Islam understands itself as the religion appropriate to mankind, so that its revelatory document properly fits and fulfills the human meaning. And it is no improper assumption to see it belonging, in its actual sequence, with the personal yearnings and searchings of Muhammad's own mind and spirit. There are large questions here. But the Qur'an is emphatic about itself as 'the revelation of the Lord of the worlds, with which the faithful Spirit descended upon your heart . . .'. It was not merely set upon the prophet's lips and tongue, but engaged his innermost thoughts, as the heart knows them. Such, at least, is the implication of this passage (Surah 26.192–4).

The Qur'an turns away from the covenantal basis of the Old Testament into a universally human calling under God. But it turns back also to a kind of Sinai where the divine relationship is one of law and sovereignty in which the redemptiveness that is crucial to the New Testament has no necessary place. Hence the theology differs profoundly and the prophetic, understood as finalised in Muhammad, replaces the Messianic as achieved in Christ. Yet the sense of the divine initiative, whether of covenant, or gospel, or law, is everywhere primary in these expressions of religion. The significance of revelation is that it meets and satisfies the expectancies, however varied, with which men have longed for it. Once given and established, whether in Moses, or Jesus, or Muhammad, in Torah, Gospel and Qur'an, it continues to direct and mould the expectations of its peoples. Systems of faith are the continuities of what once began. The 'words' their worship has are responsive to the words, 'the Word', believing has received.

Where those great assurances are lacking that make Jewry, the Church and Islam, or even within them in the mood of surmise and disquiet, the word of expectancy persists. 'Lord, I believe: help Thou mine unbelief.' Or, perhaps: 'Lord, I do not believe, help Thou my belief.' Walter de la Mare has caught the quality of this insistent asking in the lines:

> Son of man, tell me
> Hast thou at any time lain in thick darkness
> Gazing up into a lightless silence,
> A dark, void vacancy,
> Like the woe of the sea
> In the unvisited places of the ocean?
> And nothing but thine own frail sentience
> To prove thee living?
> Lost in this affliction of the spirit,
> Didst thou then call upon God
> Of his infinite mercy to reveal to thee
> Proof of His presence
> His presence and love for thee,
> Exquisite creature of His creation?
> To show thee but some small devisal
> Of His infinite compassion and pity,
> Even though it were as fleeting
> As the light of a falling star in a dewdrop?[4]

'Quiet yet unquiet waiting', Franz Kafka once called it,[5] and the unquietness comes not only from the wondering, but from the accusing. That upturned face we noted in the imagery of Heb. 4.13, has reason to be first averted. Deep and authentic in the 'words' of religion is the cry of reproach, Godward, for the way the world is. The angry fist, shaken at the heavens, may seem a puny futility. Yet, if it were, it could hardly happen. The search for what the old writers called a theodicy, the justification of God, is paradoxically the authentic demand of theism. For, in accusing a responsibility, it is passionately assuming one. If evil, somehow, does not *mean*, then nothing

means. The mystery of evil is not solved but dissolved, if there
is no liability to accuse.

When the whole dark tragedy of history bears down upon
our spirits we understand why people sing: 'It's God they
ought to crucify.' When Job, as we saw, was exploring where
to find God, it was that he might 'find' him in another sense,
that is, to 'order his cause before Him'. How are we to
reconcile God with what is, and what is with God?
Dostoevsky's hero found faith in God easy enough provided
one did not have to connect him with the world.[6] What, in
those terms, is easy is also empty. In the vocabulary of any
relevant faith there is bound to be the 'word' of desperation, as
well as of expectancy. Indeed, the two interdepend. The dark
shadows of faith belong with hope. There is this radical
interrogation of existence in the mood of most religions. But,
for obvious reasons, it is sorest in those that affirm most. The
monisms, shortly to be pondered, know the anguish but solve it
differently. Within the first two theisms, and perhaps it is fair
to say most of all in Christianity, it is crucial for theology.

But, if we are honest, the reproach is also in reverse. 'The
word we have to say to God' is penitence. In all Biblical and
Quranic prayer there is acknowledgement from the unworthy.
'God be merciful to me a sinner.' For 'the consciousness of sin
is the expression of absolute respect'. Isaiah's vision of
vocation (6.1–12) is the classic expression of this truth. 'Woe is
me for I am undone, for mine eyes have seen the king, the Lord
of hosts.' Such may well be the intention of the verse in Heb.
4.13. 'Him to whom we give account' may be the primary
sense of the phrase. It has to do with responding to a
reckoning. Unclean people, unclean lips, unclean thoughts.
'Seek forgiveness from God' is a steady refrain in the Qur'an. 'I
am no more worthy to be called thy son', is the hallmark of the
Christian's awakening to grace. In this sense, the day of
judgement is a perennial reality. To be aware of sin present in
the heart and to want it purged is the token of the nearness of
'Him with whom we have to do'.

Deeply personal as this emotion is, and not to be escaped by
alibis, it must not stay in a private pietism, where it could
retreat into inverted merit. It must face outward also to the

world as a penitence that wills to care, if vicariously, about collective ills. There would be some implied, or perhaps expected, exoneration of ourselves, if we were to assume that the divine reproach against us related only to our private sins. Humanity and history, as we belong with them, are beset with evils which cry to be acknowledged for the wrongs they are. But, because they are collective, pervasive, general, complex, and we ourselves anonymous, remote, detachable from their incidence by long and devious causes, we may readily, conveniently, assume our innocence. When the factors behind world poverty, the blight of malnutrition, and the urban ghetto, are so dispersable among a profusion of interests and events, we may say they are no guilt of ours. But such easy innocence itself becomes a crime, before 'the eyes of Him with whom we have to do'. Penitence, as Luther affirmed, in the first of his famous Theses on the Cathedral door, is always the first duty of Christians. And, since we are 'involved in mankind', it must be the will to heed the divine accusation of our time. Only so do we pray for the hallowing of his name.

Exploration, expectancy, accusation in both senses—these accents in 'the word we have to say' have their climax in the silence of adoration, in the awareness of the unspeakable, the light of the unapproachable. This is *Magnificat*: this, in Islam, is *Takbīr*, the confession that God is divinely great. 'Let everything that hath breath praise the Lord', interpreting the silence of wonder in the gladness of song. This call of the psalmist is the ultimate meaning of 'the word that is ours'. 'We praise Thee as God, we acknowledge Thee to be the Lord. All the earth doth worship Thee, the Father everlasting'—He to whom is the chorus of our whole being, whose glory we speak in choir and symbol, in stone and colour, in poem and chant, in the arts and with the artisans 'without whom a city cannot be inhabited ... who maintain the fabric of the world and all their desire is in the work of their craft' (Eccles. 38, 32 and 34). In and through all the themes of gratitude and praise, the word passes into that worship which is beyond all seeking and receiving. 'Blessed be God, only and divinely like Himself.'

This, so to speak, is 'the book of common prayer', the fivefold voice of search and desire, of hope and converse, of despair and quarrel, of contrition and guiltiness, of wonder and benediction—the voice of the upturned face of man. These, we may say, are the dimensions of religion, as measured, variously but assuredly, in the Semitic traditions of faith.

In measure it could also be said that they are the book of prayer common to even wider bounds of human expression and devotion. Exploration and adoration, certainly, though significantly different for the absence, or at least radical revision, of the sense of the givenness in revelation and of the reality of evil. But with these kinships of further Asia, vital as they are, it is perhaps fair to say that, for purposes of simple exposition, the religions of the east, the monisms, take us into insistent contrast with the stance of Heb. 4.13.

The trouble, frankly, is with the first word, with those vital pronouns, 'Him' and 'us', 'Thou' and 'we'. For, to Asian religion, they are inacceptable: more, they are delusory. Pronouns are not to be used in transcendental reference nor are 'us' and 'ours', 'me' and 'mine', words that can rightly relate to things beyond sense and time. Prayer, presuming to use pronouns in that way, is a habit which has quite misread the real nature of the Real and, kindred error, has misconstrued its own subjectivity. Monotheism is, at best, illusion and, at worst, a form of pride. To have understood the meaning of the Upanishads of Hinduism, or the Dhammapada, the Buddhist Scripture, is to know that such pronounal prayer, in any of the accents we have been pondering, is impossible. If man thinks of himself standing before God, in hope, or fear, or guilt, or wistfulness, or wonder, he is sadly lost in duality—a duality which must be transcended in the burning realisation of the Real. As long as we are imprisoned in pronouns we have not lost ourselves in *Advaita*, in non-dualist awareness of the negation of all particularity. We are merely making God in our own image.

It needs a careful and sustained effort of mind for the theist to penetrate this radical disqualification of himself and of his theology. One of Franz Kafka's short stories may serve us in the effort. For Kafka, with his anguished hero, in *The Trial* and *The Castle*, is often read as a superb exponent of the burden of the human meaning taken as personal. In both novels 'Joseph

K.' has a search more desolate than Job's, striving to understand his guilt, his duty, his misery, his hope, to find the ever elusive clue out of the labyrinth of his experience and never granted the answer, the assurance, which would give him peace, yet for ever unable to forbear the struggle and the quest. He represents, in perhaps more utterly tormented form than any other portrayal, the felt absurdity of contemporary man and Kafka seems to mean to have it so.

But could it be, even against his own intense dismay, that he is suggesting something else—that the search is vain because the clues are wrong, that this anguished personalism has got it wrong? In 'An Imperial Message', among his *Short Pieces*, Kafka, with a 'so the story goes', sets a stage for the futility of theism.

> The Emperor . . . has sent a message to you, the lone individual, the meanest of his subjects, the shadow that has fled before the Imperial sun until it is microscopic in the remotest distance, just to you has the Emperor sent a message from his deathbed.

The 'deathbed' sounds ominous and 'the lone individual' fits the individual identity exactly.

> He made the messenger kneel by his bed and whispered the message into his ear; he felt it to be so important that he made the man repeat it into his own ear. With a nod of the head he confirmed that the repetition was accurate.

The prophetic tradition, with its confidence in 'guidance sent'? It looks like an irony on 'revelation'. In the event, the messenger, having taken leave, thrusts his way forward on his errand, demanding passage for his all important word. But

> . . . the throng is so numerous: there is no end to their dwelling places . . . still forcing his way through the chambers of the innermost palace, he will never get to the end of them. . . .

Stairs, courtyards, more stairs, more courtyards 'and so on for thousands of years', and then all the breadth of the capital city to traverse, 'overflowing with the dregs of humanity'. A world too populous to penetrate—is this the symbol of the 'me' mentality, insisting forlornly on the 'word' from Him, which can never find me as a 'separate'?

No one could force a way through that, least of all with a message from a dead man.

Then, to conclude the 'short piece', comes the enigmatic comment:

But you sit by your window and dream it all true, when evening falls.[7]

Is that to say that the theistic illusion, nevertheless, persists, but only as a hollow dream? Or is it to hint of another pattern, beyond pronouns about a celestial 'He' and a personal 'me'—a pattern where the striving self and the futile 'Emperor' are left behind, where 'the eye goes not, nor the mind'? Kafka was aware of Taoist doctrine and seems to have felt its fascination. It is perhaps no surprise that a most haunting voice of existential despair can also be understood renouncing, if only elusively, the personal equation where despair belongs.

What may be no more than hint in Kafka is doctrine in the classic scriptures of Hinduism and Buddhism. Of course we find those classic texts using pronouns. There is the familiar *Tat tvam asi*: 'That Thou art', or 'Thou art that', of the Asian faiths, the name of the *Brahman/Atman* or 'truth beyond truth'. But pronounal speech here is simply the necessity of language which, clearly, we cannot avoid but which must not be taken as in any way sustaining the situation it seems to imply (namely the actuality of inter-personal relationship). For that situation is itself the reach of the illusion. We have to use the language of 'ordinary' existence to deny its suppositions.

The self-consciousness of the empirical self has to be distinguished from the *atman* of the real self, that 'the "I am" conceit may be rooted out'.[8] In Buddhism, and many forms of Hinduism, this means a radical revolution in our understanding of what it is to *be*. The very experience of physical embodiment, wherein we look out from behind our own two eyes, is as transient as any of our relationships with matter and things.[9] Those physically located senses, which turn us outward to phenomena and seem to belong inwardly with a responsible *persona* acting in a realm of meaning, in reality merit no such interpretation. On the contrary, if we take them so, we distort, as Vedantist Hindu thinking sees it, the truth of their *jiva* quality, their flux within the soul of all things, the supreme, infinite, unimaginable, imperishable *Brahman*, of which we can only say: 'Not this, not that'. To think individuation real within that universal soul is to forfeit real being in illusion and privation.

The Buddhist doctrine of *Anatta*, or not-self, is more rigorous, denying the clue of selfhood whether in the sphere of the human or of the transcendent, denying it, that is, in any concept of being, though caring for it compassionately within the diagnosis which altogether disallows its relevance. Man, as the Buddhist interprets him, is caught in *samsara*, the flux of illusory existence in the conditioned world. *Dukkha*, impermanence and unreality, suffering, are here his portion. These he must escape or, better, supersede, by achieving a soul-theory in the acceptance of which grief, sorrow, distress, privation, and the like, could no longer obtain, because he has transcended the desire on account of which he is a prey to these. Desire has this malign quality because, within it, there is a *karma* (from the root 'to do') which, as 'volitional action', contrives to maintain the will to be and, with it, the will to these privations. This entailing, or persistence, of 'desire' passes on beyond the death of the 'volitioner'. Its abating takes a prolonged discipline. For its consequences are not readily dispelled. But, as *Tanha*, or 'drives', are broken, the thirst to be is shed and *Nirvana* is attained. The goal is not another 'something', but the realisation, beyond both existence and non-existence, of the true state where impermanence has at length been defeated and unmasked. What might seem like atrophy, if one took the self for real, is liberty when one knows it as illusory—'the unborn, the not-become, the not-made'. Then there is no more coming to birth, no more ageing, no more dying. For it was the sick man, the old man, the dead man, as the Buddha met them in his foray from the palace, who remain the final clue to the Buddhist understanding of the human situation. That which is doomed, by nature, to sicken, weary

and die, cannot be the real. Transience argues unreality.
'Desire not to desire' must, therefore, be the answer to the
mystery. 'Happy indeed the *Arhants*! In them no craving's
found. . . . Lust-free, they have attained. . . .'[10]
This utterly radical alternative to the sense of the self in man
as theism sees him has its counterpart for Buddhism in the
utter incongruity of notions of creation and a creator deity.
Hinduism has been able and willing to contemplate the
Ishvara, or one uncreated world ruler, capable of diverse forms
and compatible with manifold deities and *devas*. But
Buddhism, except in minority moods, sees karmic conditioning
as inward to itself. There is no eternal Self as the cause of the
world. Karmic law and divine *fiat* cannot logically coexist.
Given *karma*, God has no function to fulfil. Indeed, the
Buddhist can go further and undertake to explain how the very
idea of creation arose. Within the multiplicity of the karmic
universe-forces, *brahmas*, powers, themselves perpetually
derived and deriving, developed the illusion of some initiatory
primacy by which they saw themselves 'original' and the
sequent things their 'creatures'. But this theology is all of one
piece with the illusion of the selves of creatures. The two
illusions, mistakenly but understandably, corroborate each
other, as, indeed, theists declare, with their sturdy 'I/Thou'
convictions about man and God.

Some would want to argue that this quite uncompromising
rejection of theism on the part of Buddhist philosophy can be
somewhat softened. It can be pleaded that the Buddha did not
himself pronounce atheistically, that he was essentially a
guide, the guide, to self-liberation. It is also perhaps feasible to
argue that *Nirvana* replaces God in the Buddhist scheme. But,
significant as these considerations are, especially the hint in
them that we might hearken to the psychology of guidance
without the ontology of karmic flux, they remain marginal to
the text of the Buddhist Scriptures. It is sounder, at least in this
context of the dimensions of religion, to let the conflict stand.

We are here a long way from the alertness of Heb. 4.13.
'Him with whom the word is ours' has become 'that wherein is
undesiring'. It is perhaps pointless to try to reconcile the two,
though, for example, T.S. Eliot sought to do so.

> Desire itself is movement
> Not in itself desirable;
> Love is itself unmoving,
> Only the cause and end of movement,
> Timeless and undesiring
> Except in the aspect of time
> Caught in the form of limitation
> Between un-being and being.[11]

Meanwhile,

> ... the world moves
> In appetency, on its metalled ways
> Of time past and time future.[12]

It would be trite to plead that the formula might be: 'Desire a right desiring', rather than the paradoxical 'Desire undesiring'. Then, despite that impermanence that none can deny, the significance of personal love might return, more warily indeed, but no less surely, as the open secret and the upturned face.

There is risk, of course, in condensing the vast, bewildering, intricate complexity of Asian religion into the simple elements of this discussion. It deserves better of our patience and our subtlety. But enough is clear to indicate its contrasted measure of the nature of religious man. Early in the nineteenth century, the German philosopher, Schopenhauer, rejoiced that his

> ... still young century ... had been allowed access to the Vedas through the Upanishads ... I suspect [he added] that the influence of Sanskrit literature will be no less profound than the revival of interest in the Greek was in the 15th century.[13]

'Europe invaded by Asia'[14] is no doubt overstating the fulfilment Schopenhauer's anticipation has found in our own time, but this parallel with the Renaissance at least suggests the range, if not the impact, of what the questing, striving, bustling, querying west has to recognise in the eastern dimensions of religion.

One sobering, yet heartening, observation which emerges for the student of this contrast between pronounal and non-pronounal faiths is the nostalgia (if it might be so described) which seems to grow within either for the other. Hinduism, of course, is rich in personal piety and *bhakti*-style devotion to a variety of deities, availing to bring the warmth of pronounal love within the soul, but always penultimate to the mystery beyond them which they may not displace, except thus ritually. Buddhism, for its part, develops the deep changes of temper which divide the rigorous Hinayana from the Mahayana. The Buddha's compassion, in the latter, is not only that of the historic founder summoning disciples to the stern regimen of undesiring. It proceeds through the manifestations of the Eternal Buddha, generating joy and love for *dharma* and so aiding mortals, somewhat in the manner of the grace in Christianity.[15] The sense that even this is still illusory, a concession only to the frailty of man, persists when Buddhism is truest to its temper. Yet, however we may explain it by influences from Hinduism or from Christianity,[16] it indicates, beyond all its tensions with the pure *dharma*, a 'desire' within the undesiring.

Such fascinating evidence of the interpenetration of religions brings us, directly, to the themes of mysticism. For there even the most disparate discover some affinity. Mysticism tends to divide quite evidently into monist and monotheist and so betrays within itself the broad religious dichotomy we are studying.[17] Yet, by the same token, it conjoins them. We find in Islam, for example, the most urgent insistence that 'I/Thou' must be transcended in the single union which is the mystical meaning of Islamic *Tauhīd*. This term, which for the orthodox means affirming categorically that 'God, He is One', means for the Sufi the experience of *fanā*', or ecstatic annihilation, in which the self is lost in the One.

> In his divine majesty 'I', 'thou' and 'we' shall not be found. 'I', 'thou', 'we' and 'He' bear the same meaning, for in unity there is no division. Every man who has annihilated the body hears within his heart a voice that crieth: 'I am God.'[18]

Or, in the lines of the poet, Jami:

> Beware! say not: 'He is all beautiful

And we His lovers.' Thou art but the glass
And He the face confronting it, which casts
Its image in the mirror. He alone
Is manifest and thou in truth art hid.
Pure love, like beauty, coming but from Him,
Reveals itself in thee. If, steadfastly,
Thou canst regard, thou wilt at length perceive
He is the mirror also, he alike
The treasure and the casket. 'I' and 'Thou'
Have here no place, and are but fantasies,
Vain and unreal.[19]

There are many comparable passages in the literature of Christian mysticism. Just as Buddhist instincts hold loyalties in line, so there are reservations, except among the boldest within monotheism, about whether their mystical experience takes them into non-pronounal unity. Islamic mysticism, for example, contains a long debate as to the unitive state. If, as was often the terminology, ecstasy could be described under the figure of wine and its inebriates, then was there a deeper 'sobriety', beyond, of course, the normal soberness of the unawakened and the uninitiated who had never sought the mystery, yet also leaving the ecstasy itself in returning to the daily world?[20] Was the self given back to itself, illuminated and apprehended truly, but still an 'I' for whom there would ever remain 'the wholly Other', the divine 'Thou'? Jalāl al-Dīn Rūmī, the master-poet of Muslim religion, seemed to feel so, if not always unambiguously.

Awhile, as wont may be,
Self I did claim:
True self I did not see
But heard its name.

I, being self confined,
Self did not merit,
Till, leaving self behind,
Did self inherit.[21]

Here, we are not far from the Gospel's: 'He that loveth his life shall lose it, but he that loseth his life for my sake, the same shall find it' (Matt. 10.39 and John 12.25), if we understand the poem to mean the self-surrender that cancels selfishness, not the self-annihilation that makes selfhood to cease.

Far as these alternatives reach, there is a common theme in the mystical experience through every varied hinterland of doctrine or of culture where it has its home. That fact goes some way to keeping open the avenues of relevance between systems which, in their isolation, would appear irreconcilable. It is this which makes important the meeting of persons—rather than the sharp comparison of -isms—for which a plea was made in Chapter 2. Such openness, however, will not of itself resolve the content, though it may greatly help the temper, of the crucial differences that persist.

Some may like to conjecture whether the *Advaita*, non-duality religions, are, so to speak, a half-way house on the way to the realisation that the bliss of their goal is, veritably, God as Love, where the language of persons is no strange music. Then they might find themselves asking, within the compassion they know so carefully, the question of Browning's David in the presence of the broken Saul:

> Do I find love so full in my nature, God's ultimate gift,
> That I doubt his own love can compete with it?
> Here, the parts shift?
> Here the creature surpass the Creator. . . .
> Would I suffer for him that I love?
> So wouldest Thou, so wilt Thou. . . .[22]

Or, conversely, shrinking from such a forbidden and dishonouring conclusion, Asian monisms, for their part, may see the theisms as half-way houses still lacking the courage to break their too human tether and complete the path of nothingness into the beyond-desire.

But such mutual recognition, dubious modicum as it is, will seem pointless to the rigorous in either camp, and no more than a gesture of goodwill. Maybe both need to take further stock of the contemporary mood that dismisses both. For there are nouns and verbs as well as pronouns and these may provide a better clue. Religions, in the dimensions of this chapter, whether affirming or escaping 'I/Thou', are alike preoccupied with inwardness. They are ways of salvation. Suppose such salvific concern is misinformed. Suppose we take the nouns as primary—matter, natural history, society, culture, race—as biology, biochemistry, sociology, Marxism and the rest explore them. These, the nouns of space and time, are perhaps the real denominators, where religion, too proudly, too anxiously, proceeds from consciousness as such. Maybe decay is just decay; death is just death; life, despite impermanence, just life; and all things the epiphenomena of matter, needing no other interpretation.

Suppose our divergent, *religious*, views of the world and man, Semitic and Vedantist, Christian and Buddhist, are alike to be discounted, that creation-revelation-theology is a doomed reliquary of lost days of faith, that—though Hindu Buddhist religion possesses some interesting techniques—they can well be heeded without the formidable array of speculative puzzlement in which Asia loved to set them. Reduce creation–salvation legends to the plain aloneness of man in the universe, which just *is* and no inquiry: How? Accept impermanence without surrendering desire or straining to double-cross oneself into infinity.

Such are the secular conjectures, often brooding in past centuries, and current in our day, suspicious as it is of the pretensions of religions, of their escapism, and of their instinct to be over-serious or under-honest. For the present let the issues stay. No faith can be in dialogue unless it is steadily and radically exploring itself. There is a Christian attempt at this in the chapter following. It will aim to take more deeply the comparative criteria considered in this one. It will do so in the conviction that 'He with whom the word is ours' has taught us in the Word the language we may use. But it is a literacy in Christ, learned and spoken in the common world.

> Those who believe they believe in God, but without passion in their heart, without anguish of mind, without uncertainty, without doubt, and even at times without despair, believe only in the idea of God, not in God Himself.[23]

4 'The Measure of Christ'

THE theatre is not a word one readily associates with the New Testament. But, in 1 Cor. 4.9, Paul describes the apostles as 'a theatre for the world'. He has in mind the trials and adversities which make them, as he puts it, 'a spectacle to angels and men'. But those humiliations were in a larger cause. So the phrase may be rightly borrowed to serve the imagination in the comprehending of the whole New Testament. See the founding events of Christianity as a drama, its central document as world-theatre. The poet, Robert Herrick, has the thought, when he says of Jesus:

> The Cross shall be thy stage; and Thou shalt there
> The spacious field have for Thy theater.
> ... Thou art He
> Whom all the flux of nations comes to see.[1]

The hunger for action which 'the empty space'[2] of the theatre generates, the anticipation, the climax, the cleansing catharsis flowing from the action, the participation where the audience involves itself—all these may be seen to be lively parables of the hope of history, the yearning for the act that has to be, the meaning in its immediacy, and the reach of recognition by which it is possessed to the far bounds of the audience. Drama, rightly disciplined, may be the surest analogy for the Gospel. To employ it is the purpose here, taking up, as we do so, the several senses of the phrase in Heb. 4.13, used in the previous chapter, and seeing them, with the help of this image of the New Testament as a theatre, fulfilled and realised in Jesus as the Christ. Was not: 'That which we have heard ... seen with our eyes ... looked upon, and our hands have handled ...' another apostle's description of 'the word of life'? (1 John 1.1).

The empty space, as Peter Brook writes of it, is where what he calls 'the holy' happens. 'It is all very well', he says

> ... to use crumbs of Zen to assert the principle that ... every manifestation contains within it all of everything, and that a slap on the face, a tweak of the nose or a custard pie are all equally Buddha. All religions assert that the invisible is visible all the time. But here's the crunch. Religious teaching—including Zen—asserts that this visible–invisible cannot be seen automatically. It can only be seen given certain conditions.... Holy art is an aid to this, and so we arrive at a definition of a holy theatre. A holy theatre not only presents the invisible but also offers conditions that make its perception possible.[3]

That last statement is uncannily close to what the Christian faith has always believed about the nature of the history within the Gospel.

But we must begin with the emptiness, the waiting stage: it is the emptiness, not of negation, but of expectancy, of anticipation, of a human audience waiting where they are for what the situation in front of them looks meant to experience. The vacant place is the place for an answer, for an enactment by which hope's logic and yearning might be met. That place for an answer is the significance of the Old Testament, or—not to use Christian terminology—the one covenant, the Torah. The answer, itself variously anticipated, is the Messianic action by the bearer of the Messianic identity.

The history of biblical Israel, through the Law and the prophets, issues into this expectancy. Perhaps it sounds arbitrary to begin here. Why Israel, why the Old Testament, so called? Does not this particularity have to justify itself? It does so in the sequel. A particular beginning is inescapable in any religion, as in any philosophy. One cannot start presuppositionless. What matters is that the point of departure fulfils itself in where it leads. To end authentically is to vindicate one's beginning, and this is what the Christian claims of his Old Testament indebtedness. The Jewish expectancy holds, in the form of hope, all the vital elements of faith. Creation is there as a divine liability for the world, implicit in a

divine intention for it. History is there, inasmuch as its
wayward story is taken honestly. That waywardness has
within it the deep meanings of land and people on which the
Old Testament, with its memory of exodus and its conviction
of election, is built. Land and people, in their biblical
partnership, in the priestly kingdom and the royal priesthood,
are the elemental factors in all human culture and economy.
The Torah, assuming territory, belonging with people,
transacted in history, shrined in memory and ritual, both
symbolises and intends the divine human co-action, whereby
'glory may dwell in our land'. 'I will be their God and they will
be my people' in this down-to-earth, open-to-heaven, kind of
real being. There can be little doubt that this Old Testament
anthropology, exemplified in one community, essentially
translatable to all, summarises wonderfully the destiny of man
and does so, as the Bible indicates, for the benediction, the
congratulation, of all nations, blessing themselves in the God
of Abraham.

If the vocation is splendid, so is the venture grim. The
Torah, in historical experience, suffers the obduracies of its
human partner. Hope is monotonously deferred. Vocation
abides to challenge obedience but the generations in their
sequence fail it. Land and people are finally sundered in exile
and the tragic dimension emerges unmistakably within the
story. The Torah continues faithfully to summon to its
purpose, but its very constancy spells a steady accusation. The
Law, linking back through history to creation, seemed
strangely frustrated in its ill-cast hero, man. Had not Moses, in
the beginning at Sinai, descended with it into the obscene folly
of the golden calf? True, he had been summoned anew into the
cloud to receive the Law afresh. For the Law, rooted in the
God of hope and patience, does not weary of mankind, and
Moses may not stay in the gesture of despair, shattering the
tablets.

But how is that persistence of the Law's claim, of the
Torah's patience, to avail in the lengthening centuries, when
the test is not with a rabble in the wilderness, but with people,
monarchy and priests, and temple, in the long tradition of the
land?

It is here that significance deepens into the meaning of the prophets. For they, at their surest, are the mentors of the people under the Law, the steadfast remembrancers of the Torah, calling the nation to its true destiny. That vocation, in a way that casts its import forward to the future, makes them inevitably sufferers. For the perversity which resists the Law's claims, reproaches the Law's spokesmen. The enmity is transferred from the message to the messenger. This is the prophetic hazard, as it emerges most tragically of all in the career of Jeremiah, 'whose pain is perpetual and his wound incurable' (Jer. 15.18). Steadfastness inevitably incurs this sorrow of heart, these wounds. For to elude them would require silence and abandonment of the word. Equally, suffering is the entail of loyalty from yet another angle. Resistance, force, power, rather than compromise of silence, might be the prophet's answer to the obdurate. Compel them to conform. But such militancy distorts the truth. The perverse resist because, they say: 'This man is our enemy, a threat to us, to our traditions and our way of life.' If, then, the prophet invokes violence, he vindicates their saying, forfeits his ability to proclaim a pure word and loosens the descending spiral of enmity and hate in which the word is overborne. Hence the defencelessness of the great prophets in the Old Testament tradition. On every count, fidelity stands in pathos, and suffering is the hallmark of the love of truth. In all this, prophets become, as the Church was later to learn itself to be, both sign and instrument. Prophethood itself passes from speech to character, from preaching to personality. It even becomes autobiographical. The word, we can truly say, becomes a man who is its token and its vessel, by *being how* he is as well as in his *saying what* he speaks.

Putting these two dimensions together, the Law in its unrealised, yet undefeated, intention, the prophets in their double representation of the divine concern, we come to the hope of the Messiah. Truly, this theme is large, manifold and controversial—naturally so, since ideas of Messiah are a crucial element in what Messiah has to save. But, without doing violence to its whole complexity in Israel's history, it is fair to claim that there is an empty place, felt and interpreted from within the heart of that history, the place for the answer that satisfies 'within the conditions that make its perception possible'.

It is here that the Christian turns to the ministry of Jesus. To the outsider this, like an earlier beginning with the Bible, may seem arbitrary. Why make Jesus so central to one's criteria, unless one can somehow be sure that they are appropriate to God? Is not assuming them so, to beg the whole question? Or, perhaps, alternatively, the whole question *can* be identified here, in the elements with which, in Jesus, we are confronted? And anyway, is not the legitimacy, here as often elsewhere, one that we can only find in the proceeding? 'Believe in God, believe in me . . .' (John 14.1) are clauses that can depend either way round. At all events, we begin with Jesus, content to let our justification wait for us.

And we begin with his teaching and his active compassion—features which have so attracted even those who disavowed the verdicts of faith. Jesus of Nazareth stands very clearly in the prophetic sequence. 'This is Jesus the prophet of Nazareth of Galilee', his admirers said, possessively (Matt. 21.11). There is every interpretative reason to hold together indissolubly the life and the death of Jesus, the word and the personality. If he had not taught as he did he would not have suffered as he did, and as he suffered still he taught.

For the pattern we have noted in the old prophets, and which generated the image of 'the suffering servant'—be he person, community, or a fusion of both—began to be evident in the gathering confrontation of Jesus and the human constituency of his ministry. It is not that some subsequent animus of his disciples in their dispersion read unwarranted issues and hostilities into his record. The tensions lie too deep and belong too closely with the human story. It is that the transparent truthfulness of his invitation and of his accusation of unrighteousness engendered a contradiction against him of vested interest, pride of place and hardness of heart—the elements of human self-love shaping their familiar patterns of enmity. The Gospel calls these 'the sin of the world' and, by its emphasis and shape, presents them, not as the unique culpability of a particular age or people, but as the expression, there and then, of the humanity of every time and folk.

To listen, then, to Jesus' teaching about the kingdom of God, the joy of man in nature, the liberty of divine Sonship, the trust of the divine purpose, and about the distorting evils of establishment prestige, of religious scruple divorced from compassion, of hypocrisy, was to become aware of a gathering crisis of rejection. It was to witness, maybe without the vital clues, the sort of drama for which prophetic precedent lay close to hand, only that it was sharpened by the Messianic theme which belonged so closely with the confrontation. What, in the paragraphs to follow, we had better think of, to avoid confusion, as 'the Christic' steadily emerges into decision in the career and in the mind of Jesus. It is a decision which means the Cross.

In this summary context, it is not possible to do justly by all the questions of scholarly interpretation and debate which belong at this point. But to take here 'the measure of Christ' it suffices to keep in single focus the charisma of ministry, the forthrightness of word, and the grace of character, to draw into one focus the climax of suffering. For these, like the blood-stained coat of Joseph, are 'woven from the top throughout'. Through them, certainly as paradigm and perhaps also as incentive, runs the pattern of the prophets' sign and instrument, the hallmark of the man of God.

It is here that we reach what Christian conviction understands to be the divine Sonship of Jesus—here, that is, in point of history. For if the history is rightly read, its explanation is in, and from, eternity. The faith of the Incarnation, that is, of Jesus as Christ the Lord, comes to be, not by mere assertion, by adoption of a formula, by romanticism, but by recognition. Christology belongs, not first with definitions, but with decisions, not with credal status but with love in suffering. Jesus, as faith reads him, sees the Messianic task as 'bearing the sin of the world', as his ministry incurs it, and faith, still reading him, takes that task accomplished as expressive of the divine nature.

Messiahship, as the many anticipations thought of it, need not argue more than agency, more than human means. But somehow, in the shape of Jesus' achievement of it, the New

Testament reads the divine presence as though to say that the task is properly God's. That conviction takes us right back to the mystery of creation, to 'a faithful creator' whose purpose holds, in 'the Son of his love'.

Sonship, then, before it becomes a term in creeds, is a reality in deeds. We have to read that central decision of willingness to suffer (against all rival suggestions, zealot, apocalyptic, political) as the expression, in the actual, of that by which it was sustained in the volitional. 'The cup which my Father has given me...': 'Father, glorify thy Name...': 'Father, forgive...': 'Father, into thy hands I commend...'—these were the prayers within which Jesus suffered. Sonship, in that immediate, existential sense, was the context of his doing. Therefore, we take it also as the secret of his being. If Jesus is 'Son of God' in the music of the *Te Deum* and in the confessions of Nicea and Chalcedon, it is because he was the Son of God beneath the olive branches of Gethsemane, and in the darkness of Golgotha.

This faith, then, is not of some strange figure, purporting to be human and only thinly disguising a divine omniscience loosely allied with the natural. For such a faith would be merely the credulous with the incredible. That 'Jesus is Lord' means that the '...of God' which faith had earlier learned to say of men, of prophets, of wisdom, of will, could now be perfectly conjoined with the human because it had, indeed, been so conjoined in a history perfectly related to the divine mind. That confession did not, could not, mean adoption, or deification, or divinisation. For it could not be rightly stated except as the divine initiative. Questions are not rightly asked about the Incarnation which begin by misstating it. An acquired Sonship is not a fulfilled one. Only as we can say: 'God was in Christ' can we rightly say: 'Jesus is Lord.'

It is the Christic in Jesus which 'gives' us the Father. 'To have the Son is to have the Father also.' It is this Lordship, historically proven in the suffering Jesus, and eternally divine, which the Resurrection celebrates and declares in the victorious quality of the love that 'bearing all things, never fails'. As event and symbol in one, it is the truth by which the disciples are enabled to identify and rejoice in the Messiahship wrought in the Cross. The whole, in cosmic sense, is a 'theatre for the world' which both 'presents the invisible' and 'also offers conditions that make its perception possible'. As the Christian sees it the great empty place at the heart of history, 'waiting for the revealing of the sons of God', has been duly filled.

What, then, so enabled, are the perceptions that happen? Classic drama—to keep with our single metaphor—meant catharsis, or cleansing. Tragedy, as it were, purged the spectator of pride, saved him from pretension and 'presumptuous sins'. (We shall return, for another reason, to this idiom in Chapter 6.) The Gospel, in its different sense, from the beginning saw in Jesus crucified and risen the great catharsis of the world. 'Unto Him who loved us and loosed us from our sins', they sang (Rev. 1.5). Faith has richly and resourcefully perceived and told that meaning, sensing in the Cross the secret of a pardon as full as our deepest wrongs, on the condition of a penitence such as it commands. All the old vocabulary of the cultic sacrificial system lay to hand to speak its mystery. But the reality of the Cross transcends these terms even in fulfilling them. It was seen to be itself the perfect sacrament in history of that power by which alone, in the end and in the whole, evil is redeemed.

So perceived, it is also known to be all embracing. The New Testament is new in its making obsolescent the distinction between Jew and Gentile. The Fourth Evangelist has this, he feels, from the lips of Jesus himself. 'I, if I be lifted up, will draw all men unto me' (John 12.32). Not, clearly, a universally successful salvation: for that would be to override the precious freedom of the soul: but a universally accessible salvation, where accident of birth, in the ethnic sense of Sinai, or in the cultural sense of Aristotle, would not determine life in Christ. 'Thou hast opened the kingdom of heaven to all believers'—to Jew and Greek, with their different reasons, an impossible largesse. For faith, unlike race or elegance, remains within the reach of all.

Forgiveness and the openness of grace to all humanity mean, too, that the search for theodicy is answered. To have, within history, that event in which the full quality of human waywardness is present means that despair cannot have further evidence for us beyond what we have already known. If, in turn, that inclusive quality of evil has been suffered, borne, and mastered by a love thus recognisably divine, then the deepest theodicy is ours for the receiving—and all the truer in that history contains it before theology construes its reassuring logic. 'Herein is love . . .': 'Nothing shall be able to separate us from the love of God . . . in Christ Jesus our Lord' (1 John 4.10, Rom. 8.39). All that accusation of the divine which we briefly pondered in the previous chapter is countered in the Cross, not by suppression, not by dismissal, nor by intimidation, which may have been the case with Job of old, but by a love which takes the onus and so draws the sting. The meaning of God in Christ through the Cross is that we are warranted in believing that he is consistently, in all the things we cannot understand, what here we have perceived him to be. This is the ultimate and, for us now, the only necessary, theodicy.

What, then, of participation—that other dimension of the dramatic situation? Is there, does there not have to be, as it were, the reflex action of those who take it in? Just as the prophet in Isa. 53 finds himself altogether identifying with the figure he describes: '*Surely* he has borne our griefs . . .' so we, gathered round this fact of our redemption, find we cannot state it without personal pronouns. Indeed, this, we might say, is pronounal religion in the utmost sense. 'The Son of God loved me and gave himself for me': 'My soul doth magnify the Lord, my spirit has rejoiced in God my Saviour' (Gal. 2.20, Luke 1.46–7). By its very nature the fact of Christ crucified and risen incorporates, in mind and soul, the apprehending world. This happens in three realms—the Scriptures, the Church and the Eucharist. For these are the documentary, the institutional and the liturgical perpetuation of the Christ-event. Interdepending as they do, they possess, as book and people and celebration may, the continuity of the Christic reality that gives them being.

'In the beginning was the writing' is what the Evangelist did not say. First the Word, as person, then the words as record. The New Testament is, characteristically, Gospels and

Epistles. The former are not 'lives' of Jesus. Rather, they give access to his Christhood, as word, and character, and ministry and suffering achieved it. They are written from within the church of the Epistles, those apostolic documents of Christian education in which the community of faith is steadily initiated into the meaning of its discipleship by meeting the issues of daily living in the pagan world. Hence the local quality, the specifics of circumstance, the typical nature of this collection of letters, full of definitive precedents, yet all the time proceeding. These lesser precedents of Corinthian liberty, Philippian joy, Galatian temptation, Colossian 'mystery' and the rest, are only more particular items of the supreme and inclusive education by precedent which is the motif of the Gospels in documenting 'the mind of Christ'.

There are many issues for study in the relation of document to community and of document to history in New Testament scholarship. It could hardly be otherwise. Is it not participation we are studying? Does the audience always get it right? Or do historians? For 'history' written is always interpretatively joined with 'history' occurring. There is what happened and there is what what happened meant. The 'history' is deeply 'right', as and when the interpretation, integral as it must be to history at all, has truly apprehended. A Christian position here, in respect of the New Testament, is one of sober, critical confidence. It holds that 'the mind of the Christ' generates the mind of the Church about the Christ, and not the other way round. However far the circumstances in the days of the writing affected the nuances of the content of what was written, it seems clear there would have been no writing had not the fact generated and controlled it.

So it is that down the centuries the New Testament renews, as far as record can, a steady partaking in the history that made it. But not in mere perusing. The Scriptures are themselves the fruit of fellowship. Letters are necessary because people disperse: Gospels come to be because time moves and generations pass. The Canon which makes them definitive for faith is itself an act of communal mind. More deeply still, the making one of Jew and Gentile, in Christ, means a new dimension of community. From Jerusalem and

Antioch the faith reaches, in centrifugal motion, for its human whole: back to Jerusalem, in centripetal compassion, comes the Gentile offering to make good the bold words about the wall of partition broken down (Eph. 2.14). No longer land-tied, because no longer ethnic, this new 'people of God' is instinctively organic, corporate, not an isolated collection of private believers but a body linked and knit together and heir, as such, to all the sign-and-instrument quality which Judaic nationhood and Hebrew prophethood had understood.

Here, too, there are large questions for the scholar and the critic. 'Jesus announced the Kingdom of God and what appeared was the Church', wrote Alfred Loisy, clearly implying a maximum problematic.[4] It would be quite false to dismiss him out of hand. But it would be no less false to disallow that sequence, properly conceived. For if the Kingdom turns on Cross and Resurrection it as surely generates community. Only so can its significance exist.

The element of supercession, inseparable from the sense of the Church as 'the new people of God', must be carefully pondered. It is not a brusque rejection, children disowning their origins, debtors their debts. On the contrary, the Torah as the original matrix of the new, and all its history, are devoutly treasured and incorporated. The springs of history flow through the new channels. The inclusive unity in no way begins with any Gentile exclusivism. The story is entirely the reverse. If, in the pressures of the Empire, the Fall of Jerusalem, the inward security complex of Judaic culture and the *antisepsis* (so to speak) of Jewishness, ensured that Christianity became in the second century dominantly Gentile, this development is no inward logic of intention. It is, rather, with these outward circumstances and inward factors, the outworking of the Christic issues themselves. Messianic identity, in the first place, and *this* crucified identity, with, further, the receiving of the Gentiles without Sinai—these together, central as they are to the Church's reading of Jesus, are the *locus standi* of the faith and so of the faith's fellowship. The loss of the Jewish dimension, in terms, that is, of numbers, not of heritage, must be seen as the price of fidelity to Messiah according to Jesus and to his inclusiveness. The distinction between Jew and Gentile in fact proved far more stubborn, with its roots in a long ontology of people and providence, than Paul in his passionate confidence conceded. The enmity deepened over the Messiah of reconciliation. Clouded and tragic as the issue became, it is all the greater benediction to recall that in the definitive beginnings of the Christ-community, reconciliation was its charter.

Eucharist was its symbol. The grace which the Scriptures treasured and the Church experienced, the liturgy expressed. Jesus took bread, 'on the night in which he was betrayed', intimating in the setting of the ancient Passover the meaning of his Cross. 'This'—the bread and the wine—'in remembrance of him' became the 'holy art', we may reverently say, where 'perception' happens, responsive thus, poetically and truly, to the central drama of the Christ. 'We believe', wrote R. C. Moberly, in the first year of this twentieth century in one of the finest works of Anglican theology, *Atonement and Personality*:

> We believe that Calvary wonderfully includes and conditions ourselves.... It is to Calvary that ... we most earnestly desire to hold fast.... We are still kneeling to worship, with arms outstretched from ourselves in a wonder of belief and loving adoration, that reality wholly unique and wholly comprehensive, the figure of Jesus crucified.[5]

Those 'arms outstretched' are not reaching emptily towards a vision. 'Into their hands' says the simple rubric of the liturgy: 'Take this', said Jesus 'and divide it among yourselves'. The Cross of Jesus, so to speak, devises its own recognition in the community that gathers round its meaning. The redeemed must be redeemers. Here is no romantic, irresponsible salvation, private to the soul: rather it claims a commitment to its saving purpose in the world. 'It is the mystery of yourselves', said Augustine, 'that you receive'.

In one sense the holy communion was plainly unnecessary, at least as a preventive of oblivion. Jesus was altogether unforgettable. Certainly so to the disciples in the Upper Room—which is where our interpretation must begin. Anything, in mere recollection of him, was utterly superfluous: the implication that it might be necessary was surely painful, even cruel, among devoted men. It is well to make this point, if only to insist that the Last Supper has nothing at all to do with *whether* Jesus would be remembered. Why then so deliberately inaugurated with such pathos? Only, surely, to illuminate from within the coming climax, to educate the disciples, not 'lest they forget', but *how* they remember. It is the manner of memory that is decisive. Not whether but how.

By *this* ordaining, memory becomes more than bare recollection. It is *anamnesis*, living again in the night of betrayal, enacting anew, belonging with, entering into, comprehending in both the senses and the soul. Jesus, it would seem, had 'how' in mind in respect both of himself and them. Not 'in remembrance' some ceremonial recital of the Beatitudes, some ritual celebration of the Sermons, not even some careful publication of texts he never wrote. The Supper centred on the sufferings—not on the sufferings isolated from the whole, but consummating it. The Eucharist, like the balance in the Gospels, reads into a climax where the meaning clarifies.

Ceremonial recitals might simply evoke admiration, even sincere applause, from which any real commitment could well evaporate. For admiration is not what Jesus sought. Nor is patronage. His pattern of remembrance was intended to engage a total recruitment of the self of man within the framework of the once-for-all event which claimed it. This was the meaning of the bread and wine. These reached back, in their simple quality as things of earth and labour, into that covenantal trust of matter in man's hallowing which the Old Testament sense of land and people taught. They symbolised a consecration of the material order in the human use. But on that elemental truth of them came the significance of man's redemption in 'the body and the blood', in the self-giving of the Christ. That reality, taken as bread is to life, spelled faith's participation in Christ's redemption. The meal being common, unity was known. As a perpetuated liturgy, the Eucharist expressed in one sacrament the event, the faith and the togetherness that makes the Christian whole.

Its counterpart is the sacrament of baptism, the initiatory symbolism, the personal 'sign of the Cross'. Is it to these two sacraments that the Creed refers in confessing 'the communion of holy things', the *communio sanctorum*, often assumed to be 'the communion of saints'? In any event, the things, and the people, of God belong together. Baptism, too, goes back to what is elemental in nature and what is definitive in history, to the simplicity of water-washing and the drama of water-crossing, to the prosaic washtub and the biblical Rubicons at the Red Sea and the Jordan. Either way, it means the new in the fabric of the old, whether the garment cleansed or the people liberated. Baptism, too, bespeaks Christian personalism with a telling simplicity, bestowing a name and clinching an identity. Doing so, it is a strangely suggestive interparable with death. The fact that each can be the clue to the other is eloquent of both. Baptism means 'a death unto sin and a new life unto righteousness'. 'Baptised into Christ's death' was St Paul's formula (Rom. 6.3). But death, in turn, physical demise, the individual's final call to consent to cease to be—these can be comprehended as his baptism, his entry into life eternal. The physical necessity, as such, makes consent, on one level, quite irrelevant. But, consciously willed, it tallies with that steady life-surrender which has learned to say inwardly: 'You are not your own.' Perhaps there is no feature of Christian conviction quite so characteristic, conceptually at least, of its understanding of the person and its real sense of Christ, than this capacity of death and baptism to afford interpretation of each other.[6]

The Christ-event, then, is 'a theatre for the world' and Christian faith is life in the perceptions it makes possible. If the metaphor of world drama has in any way fitted us to comprehend ourselves 'in Christ', it may also have informed us for that taxing conjunction 'and' coupling 'the Christian' with 'other religion'. This was the point of borrowing it. For the criteria of our relationships must be 'the measure of Christ'. It is well to know where we are, with conviction and with humility, when we come to dialogue.

Is it possible that our surest clue in that exacting role is to look to discover every 'in Christ' quality, or feature, or accent, that can be discerned in other religion, and to do this, not possessively, and certainly not patronisingly, as if we were proprietors, but with a lively and a generous hope? Sceptics have often insisted that many elements in the Christian version of reality we have just summarised in this chapter owe themselves to pagan cults, Greek mysteries and a Roman market of ideas.[7] What we have called the Christic is not necessarily disqualified by recruiting to its interpretation the resources of the human manifold. What matters is which is determinative. If they were then recruited, may they not be sought out now? Are there clear senses in which the questions, the anxieties, the stopping-points, the conclusions, and, properly, the symbols, of other men's faith-systems have elements that are already 'in Christ', and may, by us, be recognised as such?

This possiblity takes us into the concerns of Chapter 6. Meanwhile, it is important to review, in advance of this practical task, the more general debate within Christian theology about the puzzling otherness of religions.

In Westminster Abbey there is a rose window in which great figures of the biblical tradition, patriarchs and prophets, with the apostles of Christ, appear with Socrates and Plato, masters of the Greek mind. What has our theology to say of associations wider still?

5 Beyond tolerance

WHEN he was a writer in Lahore, Rudyard Kipling was inspired to a characteristic jingle of lines by a local Lodge of Freemasons.

> We'd Bola Nath, accountant,
> An' Saul, an Aden Jew,
> An' Din Muhammad, draughtsman
> Of the Survey Office, too.
> There was Babu Chuckerbutty,
> An' Amir Singh the Sikh,
> An' Castro from the fittin' sheds,
> The Roman Catholick![1]

One sample of tolerance but, in its eclectic way, still leaving a lot of open questions.

As an alternative to persecution, antagonism and ill-will, tolerance in almost any shape is greatly to be esteemed. The path of religion has too often and too long been a way of hostility and polemic. Establishments have had to be repudiated before tolerance could prevail. Much is owed, religiously, to sceptics and agnostics. History makes it clear that religious institutions are never safe among the unquestioning. Their health needs the very temper they are prone to suspect or to suppress, namely the temper that withholds commitment.

Yet tolerance, for all its benediction, has problems of its own. It so easily degenerates into indifference, loses a fine sense of alternatives and forfeits issues in a timid apathy. Unless it is alert, it will allow illusions to persist or new conspiracies to develop against it undetected. When a supine tolerance presides negligently over things at stake, its very value is reversed. Tolerance is, therefore, never a final prescript, if only for the reason that, without positives it must require, it will find itself conniving with decline. There are also acute practical social problems inside religious themes, which make tolerance, in abstract ideal, a hollow word, until the tasks are shouldered.[2] Guardians of indifference are, plainly, a contradiction in terms. So we return to tasks of the spirit and these, again, however reluctantly, bring us back to religion.

But, in these senses, beyond tolerance—what? The question about co-existence is not whether but how? Each faith has to answer out of its own resources. In particular, how has recent Christian theology understood the tolerant role of faith? Within that question, what becomes of mission in the context of plural, mutual respect and of cohabitation in the world? What, further, have we to say of finality, authority, uniqueness and the claim to truth, which are implicit in belief in revelation, in sacred history, in the grace of Christ, and in the Holy Spirit 'proceeding from the Father and the Son' and so moving, that would seem to mean, in Christian channels? If God is not the author of confusion, why so many creeds and why the spiritual impracticability of neglecting the competitors? These, and dependent, questions arise at every point.

The situation, in a certain way, almost resembles that in ecumenical debate in the last half-century. Many church theologies had necessary, even adamant, conditions of validity of ministry, of church-status and authenticity, which were far from being everywhere fulfilled. Indeed, they were rigorously selective in their all important *Nihil obstat* verdict, matters of order, being, for this thinking, equal to matters of faith. Yet, increasingly, such attitudes were reluctant to disqualify evidence of grace in irregular form or situation, or to offend against spiritual sensitivities which seemed to be involved—not to mention practical factors. So mediating ideas developed—irregular grace, the *esse* and the *bene esse*, what the Spirit did via the channels and what, mercifully if disconcertingly, He did despite the lack of them. Only slowly did reflection suggest that perhaps the issues had initially been wrongly drawn.

Are we perhaps in a comparable situation with other faiths?

Perhaps not. Clearly it is a far sharper problem when widened beyond the discernible Christ-focus altogether. The Christ-crux of Christianity—and its absence—are far deeper issues than the ways of grace within that native ground. The parallel here in mind, if it exists, should not be pressed in expectation of any comparable development. For something much more radical is at stake. Yet—even so—*a* parallel is traceable and something like comparable suggestions emerge. Perhaps there is *the* way of grace and other ways-irregular, the baptism in fact and the baptism of desire, the explicit and the anonymous love of Christ, the obedience via Scripture and sacrament and the obedience via conscience and nature. To undertake the onus of such conjectures, and much else, is what is here meant by 'beyond tolerance'. For tolerance alone might for ever hedge these obligations.

As mission belongs so intimately with this debate, let us make it initially biographical and start with a missionary of very rare distinction, surely the only one ever to be honoured with a postage-stamp portrait by the land of his adoption in the days of independence, Charles Freer Andrews (1871–1940). He was also a near perfect portraiture of that courtesy of temper which was the concern of Chapter 2. More, he toiled actively with Gandhi for Indian liberation, education and reform. His response to Hinduism was ardent and expectant and always lively. With his colleagues in the Cambridge Mission to Delhi, he was impressed with the idea that India might play the part in Christianity which Greece had played in the days of the Fathers. Perhaps, indeed, on one reading of history, it had already played it. Andrews wrote:

I am beginning to understand from history that Christianity is not an independent Semitic growth, but an outgrowth of Hindu religious thought and life besides. . . . Christ appears to me like some strange, rare, beautiful flower whose seed has drifted and found a home in a partly alien land. India, in this as in so many other ways, is the great mother of the world's history. Christ, the Jewish peasant, lived instinctively, as part of his own nature, this non-Jewish ideal of *ahimsa*, which is so akin to Hinduism. He had the universal compassion, the universal charity, as marked in the agony of crucifixion on the sunny Galilean hills.[3] The atonement of the Cross, he said, 'must be widened out far beyond a single act of Christ, however representative'.[4] The Christic was the dimension of all-expectant faith in the holy, of every will to forgiving love. On that basis Christianity was not the antagonist, but the helper, of other faiths and it might often be right no longer to desire to win converts from them.

Given such generosity of soul, there was perhaps inevitably an ambivalence in his theology. This topic of conversion brought it out. He made it his resolute aim to ensure that no one whom he influenced ever became a Christian unless his spirit could find no rest otherwise. Gandhi's notion that no faith of one's birth ought ever to be changed, Andrews believed to be totally disloyal to the very nature of religion. But true conversion must not mean the denial of any living truth in one's first allegiance. 'I honour Paul the apostle', he said,

... when he says: 'Necessity is laid upon me.' There are clear-cut distinctions between Christians, Hindus and Muslims which cannot today be overpassed.[5]

It was partly Andrew's realism in caring for India's social problems, as well as his Christian nurture, which sustained him in that conclusion. Responding to Swami Rama Tirtha he was insistent that Vedantist *Advaita* and Christianity were incompatible. The Christian 'will never accept as finally satisfying a philosophy which does not allow him to believe that love between human souls may be an eternal reality'.[6]

C. F. Andrews's cast of mind was not such as to reach, or maybe even desire, any final theological formulation of his mission. Perhaps the nearest he came to it was in writing:

Christ has become for me, in my moral and spiritual experience, the living, tangible expression of God. With regard to the infinitude of God that lies beyond this, I seem able at this present stage of existence to know nothing that can be defined. But the human in Christ, that is also divine, I can really know: and when I see this divine beauty, truth and love in others also, it is natural for me to relate it to Christ.[7]

Whether historic Christian faith in the Incarnation belongs with an 'infinitude' of which we 'know nothing that can be defined' is a large question. But then the New Testament was not written in the midst of Hinduism. Plainly, with Andrews, spirit is willing, but problems abide.

It was such missionary experience, and other thinking in academic realms remote from travail but alert to debate, that, among other factors, inspired the forthright, yet also resilient, thought of Hendrik Kraemer, who contributed massively to the issues in the two decades after his definitive Tambaram Conference volume in 1938: *The Christian Message in a Non-Christian World*. Kraemer's kinship, though by no means slavishly, is with Karl Barth, whose position, moderating somewhat as it did, may, for present purposes, be drawn from his celebrated commentary on Romans. Ruminating on Rom. 3.22, Barth declares: 'By the knowledge of Jesus Christ all human waiting is guaranteed, authorised and established.' But this is far from the familiar 'preparation for the Gospel' stance of many thinkers earlier this century, and, indeed, of several of the Fathers. In its passionate assurance, not free from an enigmatic thrust, it seems to mean that God's waiting action, for which religions yearn, even against their own logic, is for ever concrete in Christ.

> The faithfulness of God is established when we meet the Christ in Jesus. . . . Redemption and resurrection, the invisibility of God and a new order, constitute the meaning of every religion; and it is precisely this that compels us to stand still in the presence of Jesus. All human activity is a cry for forgiveness; and it is precisely this that is proclaimed by Jesus and that appears concretely in Him. . . . In Him we have found the standard by which all discovery of God and all being discovered by Him is made known as such.[8]

Therefore, as Barth emphasises in his exposition of Rom. 1.16, 'the Gospel does not expound or recommend itself . . . it can be received and understood only as a contradiction'.[9] Elsewhere he makes sharp disavowal of any idea that the Gospel might relate to existing concepts or recognise religious relevance that has not first been subdued to the salvation categories utterly disclosed by God in Christ. Barth's theology belongs with issues of Europe, not presence in the east.

There are two points about him which we need here to keep in view. The first is the keen awareness Barth had of the sin of religions, their capacity to be themselves idolatrous, the sense in which men could well be furthest from God in the very postures of, supposedly, acknowledging him. Religious history allows us no room for naïve assumptions that piety and integrity are one. Religions have a long, dark catalogue of crimes. Barth tended to see them as necessarily condemned by the *sola fide, sola gratia*, word of the Gospel.

Secondly, that Gospel had to be radically distinguished from empirical Christianity—an emphasis that Kraemer, in turn, made strongly. It was clear to both theologians that totalitarian claims could in no way appropriately be made for the Christian institution, dogma, Church, or culture. These were not the Gospel, and lay, like other faiths, under the judgement of the Word of Christ. It is not, however, easy to see in either thinker how the Gospel could, to this radical degree, be differentiated from the Christianity that, purportedly, had it in trust, or how that Christianity could be equated, in respect of this blameworthiness of religions, with all other faiths. Surely, however unworthily, 'Christian' is, in some measure, a denominator of 'the Gospel' and vice versa? Herbert Butterfield's oft-quoted remark at the end of his *Christianity and History*, 'Hold to Christ and for the rest be totally uncommitted', is relevant here. For 'totally' is quite impossible. One only has Christ, in a properly entire commitment, by being relatively committed to much else—the Church by which one knew him, the sacraments by which one meets him, the Scriptures by which one finds him, and the culture where one lives him.[10] It is right to want to distinguish an absolute Gospel from any actual religion. But the practical impossibility of doing so may require us to call in question that sort of absoluteness, though Barth and Kraemer did not think so.

One final reflection on a Barthian-style position. Is it not likely that its insistence on a totally 'given' truth, altogether exempt from liability to relate to reason or to otherness in stating itself, and quite independent of other religions as criteria either of its meaning or its authority, is really the dogmatic form of an overwhelming experience of grace and is to be appreciated, indeed saluted and celebrated, as such? Perhaps what Barth is really saying is, in John Donne's words: 'Blessed be God only and divinely like Himself.' In which case, like Jewish assertion of unilateral chosenness—to which it is not dissimilar—we can take its positive assurance without its negative privacy.

In his *Christian Message in a Non-Christian World*, Kraemer appealed to 'Biblical realism', as the phrase was, and moved somewhat away from Barth's entire rejection of natural theology but held firmly to the view that God 'expressed clearly and exclusively in Christ's life and work His judgement on, and purpose for, man and the world'.[11] Truth in Christ and through Christ was *sui generis* because there God had willed, exclusively, to make himself known savingly to mankind and this divine action was not to be thought of as continuous with, or congenial to, the aspirations of religions. This was not to 'disregard or despise the religious life of mankind outside the Christian revelation'.[12] Quite the contrary. The point for Kraemer is that

> The Cross and its real meaning—reconciliation as God's initiative and act—is antagonistic to all human religious aspirations and ends, for the tendency of all human religious striving is to possess and conquer God, to realise our divine nature (*theosis*). Christ is not the fulfilment of this but the uncovering of its self-assertive nature: and at the same time the re-birth to a completely opposite condition, namely the fellowship of reconciliation with God.[13]

Kraemer, clearly, is formulating the issue in Christian, not, for example, Buddhist terms. He is wrestling, as Barth was, with the fallenness of religious man and absolutising, by appeal to a realism of the Bible, the answer, exempted from that fallenness, which suffices for it. On his premises, exclusivism, in Christ, is readily affirmed. But suppose we start from another angle, outside this circle of thought, can we admit the firm conclusion? Was Kraemer, at that time, too preoccupied with countering ideas of 'fulfilment' (as, for example, in J. N. Farquhar's *The Crown of Hinduism*)[14] as an account of the continuity between the tentative faiths and the final Christ, to reckon with religions more finally and with Christ more tentatively?

His deep sensitivity, born of long missionary service, nevertheless enabled him to discern and treasure 'points of contact' which, in other religions, might enable Christian communication even though they must be denied comparable status with Gospel realism. In his last work twenty years after the 1938 volume, Kraemer turned to what he called 'the coming dialogue', in his *World Cultures and World Religions*. The title, like that of its great predecessor, was significantly phrased. The author, alerted more than ever to globalism and the secular mind, was anxious to serve depth and thoroughness in the encounter which, he foresaw, could so easily be confused or even trivial in spirit. In his conclusion, he seemed to move away from the issue of truth in theology towards the obligation of truth in community.

> The meeting, the more tangible it becomes, contains inevitably many hazards, but in these hazards the opportunity arises for a salutary testing of the reality and substance of the Christian faith. The main response, however, in this dialogue is not the *thinking* but the *being* of the Church. To *be* a true Church, that is to say a Christ-centred, Christ-inspired, Christ-obeying community in word and deed, in solidarity with the world serving everybody without discrimination, is the only answer and authentication. . . . [15]

With that last word of a great Christian wrestler with the issues how cordially Andrews would agree. Yet, in a sharp way, the call to *be* the Church leaves us with the large question how to *speak* the Christ.

At the heart of it would seem to be the issue whether, contrary to Kraemer and Barth, Christian thinking must recognise that 'God is creatively, redemptively at work in the religious life of all the major communities of mankind'.[16] If so, we have to think again about how we understand and state the finality of Christ and the meaning of the once-for-all Incarnation. We have also, somehow, to relate that conviction to the sharp disparities, so evident in our thoughts in Chapter 3. It would be idle to minimise these. There is a sense, for example, in which for a sensitive Christian the Buddhist view of personality is almost a blasphemy against the Holy Spirit, the self being so preciously loved of God. Likewise God at work redemptively in Islam is a view that a cynic might feel needs some ingenuity to reconcile with the Islamic veto on a suffering Christ.

But these perplexities have to be shouldered. And, in all this, we must avoid implying divine ineptness or duplicity. Too often generous thinking, wanting to hold both options— unique grace and religious authenticity everywhere—is liable to speak to God 'trying to do things'. 'Even in this fallen world God shines through', wrote Kraemer, 'in a broken, troubled way.'[17] We need, as we shall venture to reach in Chapter 7, a right understanding of the Holy Spirit and his ways with the human scene, if we are to find our way through all these aspects of faith and diversity.

Is this conviction that God is 'creatively and redemptively at work in the religious life of all the major communities . . .' (why, one wonders, 'major' since God so loves minorities?) truly, in Bishop David Brown's phrase, 'a new threshold' Christians must cross? This 'modern Antioch' of the Church's new understanding calls, in his view, for an emphasis on the inclusive, rather than the exclusive, exposition of the Christian Gospel. His 'rather than' still leaves us with the problem of the relative weight, and of the reconciliation, of the two attitudes.

> The incarnate Christ disclosed the truth of God in such a way as to make it possible to discern and to identify God's gracious activity throughout the universe. . . . Christ did not come to make God's love and power the exclusive possession of the Church, but to reveal the nature of him who holds all things in his embrace. . . .

> Understanding other faiths in relation to the purposes of God involves a willingness to believe that many of those who practise other faiths have a living relationship with

God and know the power of his grace in their lives. It implies also a willingness to accept that they worship God as he has been made known to them, in spirit and in truth. . . . It means also to affirm that the God whom they worship is he whom Christians know as the Father of our Lord Jesus Christ, even though their understanding of his relationship with the created universe differs from that of Christians.[18]

'Crossing this threshold . . . can be a purifying and enriching experience.'[19] But suppose we are crossing it into the milieu of those for whom there is no *created* universe at all, for whom there is no '*his* grace' in other than illusory terms? Is it a threshold for the monotheisms alone? It may well be sound to appeal to the authenticity of experience, since this is the lively denominator and, in measure, the accessible one. But what of the conceptuality behind the experience? Ought this, perhaps, not to matter? Shall we be, in our very generosity, wanting the new inclusiveness still, somehow, in our own exclusive terms? Should we not, perhaps, allow religions to be different, without, of course, returning to former postures of censure or enmity? But, if we do so allow, how can we still maintain the divine that is consistent with the Christic to be at work within them? Does Bishop Brown's patient and gentle plea take us over a threshold and leave us still somewhat in a labyrinth, right as it is to step across it?

Dr John Hick of Birmingham has a more radical answer to the problem, calling it not a threshold but 'a Copernican revolution'. We need to go back to understand that the pluriformity of culture-religion we now experience began in geographical isolations, which explains why encounter with the same transcendent reality (God, not Christ is the heart of the mystery) varied, historically, so widely. Thus the One Real was diversely named, traditionally expressed, differently focused in culture. Such geographically-shaped alternatives might be likened to a planetary system around the reality of God, with thoughts of an exclusive Christo-centric truth comparable to the old astronomers' error of the geocentric universe. Even theist and monist views are somehow contained within this analogy, if we can see their disparity as reflecting aspects of the infinite encountered as personal and as Vedantist. Religions are no more rivals than planets are, having, on this view, their orbits around the single pull of the Eternal.

Even so, the earth is still lived on and, in that sense, earthly existence is truly geocentric! Similarly, the Christian lives in Christo-centric meaning. Christ is the Christian's image of God, truly worshippable but not singular. Our relationship to Christ is that of 'saved to Saviour', and the Incarnation is true in the truth of the attitude it evokes in the believer. Hick understands it as having no other truth. If, to use his verb, we try to 'unpack' the doctrine of the Incarnation we find it takes us only to our experience of Jesus as, for us, 'the way, the truth and the life'.[20]

Here are taxing problems. While it is true that the Hindu's Gita admits of the personal as supreme above the non-personal depths of *Brahman*, and Christians like Paul Tillich have spoken of 'the ground of being' where the thought of divine personality is simply the image by which being is apprehended by finite persons, these possible compatibilities of contrasted doctrines are subtle and remote from actual religion. Either/Or has a stronger case than Both/And in the theist/*Advaita* issue. As W. B. Yeats wrote in *Autobiographies*:

> In Christianity what was philosophy in eastern Asia became life, biography and drama. A play passes through the same process in being written. At first, if it has psychological depth, there is a bundle of ideas, something that can be stated in philosophical terms ... but gradually philosophy is eliminated until at last the only philosophy audible, if there is even that, is the ... expression of character. ... Was the Bhagavad Gita the 'scenario' from which the Gospels were made?[21]

Hick's explanation of religious diversities as deriving from geographical isolation also looks suspect. Planets are certainly not rivals. But did the religions have orbits? Were they not much more the neighbours of travel and war, of pilgrimage and race? Truly birth is a great determinant. But Hinduism/

Buddhism, Judaism/Christianity, Christianity/Islam, perhaps even Buddhism/Christianity, have been interpenetrating, interacting spheres of faith through much of their history and hardly any are explicable without reference to another. Traditional attitudes may long have been formed in ignorance. But they are not dispelled only by familiarity. Most important of all, Christian faith in Christ as 'Son of God' has first been faith in a historic actuality in order to be, also, as Hick rightly stresses, the Christian's proceeding upon his image of God.

'A new threshold' or 'a Copernican revolution'. Are there other ways of formulating a Christian theology that goes beyond tolerance only and into a faith about faith-diversity? The older fulfilment-into-Christ view of world religions left the question open, but it saw its ultimate conclusion already progressively assured in the inclusive Christ. To some that seemed a posture less than fully realistic, looking for the emergence of a prior assumption, and perhaps self-patronising.

Or there was the idea of reconception, developed by W. E. Hocking, for whom all religions contained, diversely, an inalienable core of truth, recognisable by human intuition and constituting a cosmic demand. Romantic syncretism should be excluded as only confounding confusion. Instead, renouncing an alternative exclusivism, each faith should strive to reconceive itself in the light of the insights it discerned in other religions. For these related to the essence of all religions. Actual faith-systems all failed to embody these insights truly. But each might aspire to do so universally, by such reconceiving. There is an attractiveness about the humility and the expectancy of Hocking's thinking.

'There is, one feels, a certain *noblesse oblige* in the relations among religions: those who have travelled far in the path of self-understanding have an obligation to those less skilled in self-explanation. Instead of using this advantage to beat their opponents down, it becomes a matter of chivalry to express for them meanings better than they themselves could express them. The joy of refutation is a poor and cheap-bought joy in comparison with the joy of lifting a struggling thought to a new level of self-understanding.'[22]

To some aspects of this we will return in Chapter 6. Like Andrews, in another idiom, its spirit is admirable. But does such spiritual chivalry to people with their ideas so readily transfer to the ideas themselves? Truly, we do well 'to anticipate for them what they mean, opening to them that larger room toward which they trend'.[23] But does this not come close to the fulfilment concept? And what if 'the trend' is our reading, rather than their nature?

Similar, in some sense, is the view that sees the divine activity present everywhere in religions, and present accordantly with the Christic as we have studied it, but present anonymously, as the Christ without the name. Nature, as understood in Christian theology, not least of the Roman Catholic tradition, is everywhere experienced. It is truly the prelude to grace. The Gospel, when it comes and when it is known, discloses the ultimate dimension, and transacts, for conscious faith, what is everywhere diffused in men's experience of life in nature. The manifest Christ articulates the latent Christ, whom men may know in genuine ignorance of the manifest. That ignorance may be such as the primitive displays. Or it may be a more subtle form, a cast of mind which, for inward reasons, conceives after a pattern that has made the Christian shape of things instinctively alien. These are, therefore, minds into which it is impossible to translate meanings, so to speak, congenitally barred. But that is not to say that, otherwise, they would not be recognised and welcomed. So, in turn, we can venture the thought of anonymous Christians. On this basis, for example, *Nirvana* may be the name of salvation and absolute transcendence read as ineffable grace.[24]

This view certainly rides with the obvious fact of the close relation between birthing and believing. But, otherwise, anonymity and faith, ignorance and grace, seem unconvincing alliances. Moreover, the situation can well be reversed and Christians become anonymous Buddhists, or anonymous Hindus, who are in invincible ignorance of the nature of non-duality, precisely because they are congenitally Christic in their thinking. There may be much chivalry in this analysis but does it really take us very far? And if we take grace back this way into nature, what do we do about regeneration and the reality of sin and waywardness? Are we not sent to preach the kingdom rather than assume it? A more consistent path would seem to be to retreat, or to advance, as the case may seem, into a full-blown mysticism as the essence of all religions, for which doctrinal issues are not a sphere of the assured or the anonymous but of the relative and the pictorial and the dispensable. But to invoke mysticism is to return back again to all the taxing problems of truth and of truth-criteria.

An interesting statement from within the Greek Orthodox tradition may be briefly noted before leaving this topic of 'extra-Christian "Christian" grace'. In 1971 in the World Council of Churches' Central Committee in Addis Ababa, Bishop George Khodr of Lebanon made a notable address, in which he spoke of the great religions within God's plan as training schools of the divine mercy. It has been a western Christian error to identify the range of the Incarnate Christ and of the Holy Spirit with the salvation history that derives from the Old Testament. There is a divine dialogue with humanity, outside the Abrahamic and the Mosaic, because of the covenant in nature with universal man. The liberty of the Spirit is not confined to the frontiers of the Church as 'the new Israel'. 'It is Christ alone', Bishop Khodr declares, 'who is received as the light when grace visits a brahman, or a Buddhist or a Muslim, reading their own Scriptures.' These extra-Christian data must be taken up into our theology. Our task is to reveal to the world of the religions the God there hidden, just as Paul, coming to Athens, found 'Christians who were not aware of their Christianity: he gave their God a name'. All that the missionary activity of the Church will ever do is to awaken the Christ who sleeps in the night of the religions. Other religions, too, exemplify even in unbelief a courageous refusal of the falsehoods which historic Christianity has been unable or unwilling to repudiate. Inclusive, not exclusive, is the right adjective for the Christian faith.[25]

As with Hocking, though with different premises, this eloquent stance leaves us practical questions to try and handle outside this chapter. As a theology, it leaves the queries already noted. Perhaps most searching of all the conjectures as to Christian duty within tolerant pluralism is that of Arnold Toynbee, who invites Christianity to heed its own summons about the corn of wheat that lives by consenting to die. This means foregoing the claim to uniqueness, abandoning exclusivism, and, allowing other faiths to be from God, sharing, as it were, a common market of the religious deeds, compassion, integrity, peace, truth. Through that openness, he believes, will come the religion that, in any sense, merits finality—a finality, not of doctrines (for these are instrumental), but of merited allegiance. The task is perennial, but currently most urgent, because of the inveterate human temptation to turn institutions into idols, not least those of religion itself.

Beyond tolerance—what? Our discussion thus far has been via people, theologians, writers, with only occasional reference, as these might choose, to the New Testament. It is fair to ask what light its text should throw upon our problems. But will it be by bare citation, whether pointing, as the passages admit, in the direction of inclusive, or of exclusive conclusions? We may cite Peter, addressing the rulers of the people in Acts 4.12, and saying, 'Neither is there salvation in any other', and assume that this is a verdict which answers all questions. Such an assumption would miss the point that he is addressing hearers who all, being Jews, share, in some sense, however disparate, the Messianic hope. He is affirming that this hope, which is their unanimous way of being saved is, in fact, realised in the crucified-reject, Jesus the Lord. Peter is disconcertingly identifying a shared hope, not prejudging an unknown Asian scene. Or there is the word of Jesus that 'no man cometh to the Father but by me' (John 14.6). Truly we come to the Father, in experience and in language, through the Son. But is this to say that no man, otherwise, comes to the Creator, to the Lord, as indeed did Abraham and the psalmist?

Or is the logos of John 1.9, so beloved of the inclusivists, 'coming into the world' to enlighten every man receiving it? Or does the participle belong to every man, so that 'entering the world' means somehow the logos light by birth? Or again, Paul at Athens—are we to argue from an unfinished speech a total

philosophy of paganism as a kind of Christianity not yet
knowing the name, or did the apostle go back on his words in
writing soon after to the Corinthians? He certainly seems to
assert an identity between the 'God' of the altar inscribed to
'the unknown' and the God of the Gospel—one subject,
differing predicates. But can we be sure?

Clearly, New Testament passages must be taken more
thoroughly than proof-texts. It seems wise to move from them
and with them as primarily a field of precedents. We find the
vocabulary of Greek, even the ideas of Stoicism in some
measure, recruited to express Christ and we find a variety of
representative situations in the Epistles which are calculated to
draw out from the apostolic mind the concrete decisions of the
faith. It is this precedent-quality of the Scriptures we should
invoke, reverently but also boldly, remembering as we do so
two facts. The one is that the Holy Spirit is never a sleeping
partner of sleeping partners, but always an active spur,
enthusing, employing, never excluding, the mind and will of
men, not purveying ready-made answers but enabling
responsible decision. Had it been otherwise, the Scriptures, as
we see them to be, could never have arrived. We need a loyalty
to them commensurate with their own origin: otherwise we
misread their authority. The second fact is that the New
Testament lives within the basin of an inland sea. It crosses no
oceans. Jerusalem round about unto Illyricum is its
Mediterranean circuit, akin to the 'letters of Greek and Latin
and Hebrew' over Jesus' Cross. It can certainly serve us in
Asia and Africa. But not if we take it merely as a blue-print.[26]

'I endeavoured to think how St Paul would act in my
situation', Henry Martyn once mused, adding, on another
occasion: 'But, above all, tell me where in Scripture I may find
India?'[27] Both, surely, fair enough questions. Add St John, too,
and China, and the lands of the Buddha and of Islam. How do
we understand the promise of the Paraclete, within the patterns
of New Testament creativity on the one hand, and within the
dimensions of the wider world on the other? Certainly we find
St Paul 'hoping to take hold of that for which Christ had taken
hold' of him (Phil. 3.12), and doing so with a lively flexibility
of mind, translating the original Palestinian faith into the

language and thought-forms of the outer world. Gnosticism, and the rest, later injected a defensive, deposit-of-faith element into that Christian trusteeship. Necessarily so. But it is the enterprise we primarily learn from the New Testament itself, a faith for ever closing with Christ and for ever opening to the future.

Even the scantiest review of recent theology of religions, like the foregoing, makes it plain that the task has still a long way to go. We must live with some bewilderment and maybe some aberrations. Continuity and discontinuity, the anonymous and the realised, waiting and fulfilment, nature and grace, are a few of the formulae to take us beyond tolerance into some rationale of Christ and the plural religions. Such a rationale, however concluded—if concluded it can ever properly be—remains discursive and conceptual. What finally matters is the relationships achieved in the actual, in the personal and the social, in the Spirit. For, whatever theory may finally satisfy the theology, the fulfilment can only be in the life.

'The love of Christ decides us', wrote Paul in 2 Cor. 5.14. If our personal position is where we staked it in Chapter 4, we must let it take us beyond the debates of this one into the active concerns of the next. We do so, readily taking a Buddhist warning about people with a faith: 'If it propounds a doctrine it must also teach the art by which we can raise ourselves to its comprehension.'[28]

6   The saving mind

'THE spirit of a sound mind', according to 2 Tim. 1.7, is the gift of God for the business of ministry, annulling 'the spirit of fear'. But the soundness the writer intends has a special quality. To reach it we have to explore the background of the term he uses. He certainly meant more than simply that lunacy was not suspected. In the tangle and tension of the interreligious issues and attitudes we have reviewed, 'a mind to save' has to inform and decide all our relationships.

The Greeks were wise enough to be often afraid of their own thoughts. So they coined the word *sophrosyne*, or safe-mindedness, to describe the sort of thinking that did not endanger the thinker. It is this term, needing an English paraphrase, which underlies 2 Tim. 1.7. Every living man is a busy rendezvous of notions and ideas, impulses, purposes, fantasies and fears, envies and conjectures. Thoughts are perpetually breeding, crowding, focusing, dreaming, intending, judging, through the life-long day of Bloom in Dublin, of everyman in his everywhere. There is no such thing as a vacant mind: only a mind in flux and mood and verdict, and, maybe, thought the Greeks, in jeopardy. Men harbour thoughts that imperil themselves—unbridled ideas, exaggerated aspirations, distorting images of themselves and others. They think proudfully, wildly, perversely. They forget their precarious mortality. They behave pretentiously and then the gods reward them with a nemesis, maybe visiting them with infatuation or fatal arrogance, working on them their own ruin.

So the urgent safety of *sophrosyne*, of safe-mindedness, the virtue which duly proportioned the mind and so preserved it from the menace of thoughts that harboured destruction in their train. The man who acquired this moderation, and only

he, was 'of sound mind'. 'Think soberly', wrote Paul in Rom.
12.3, echoing the same term and, with it, the psalmist's prayer:
'Keep thy servant also from presumptuous sins, lest they get
the dominion over me.' For tyranny, first of habit and then of
illusion, is what unhumbled thinking brings.

But is there not something lacking about this Greek security
of mind, so prudential and personal? Humility pays because
pride ruins. Modesty of mind is, no doubt, an excellent private
virtue, salting society also. But what of the thoughts that are
habitual in systems, in religious institutions, in secular patterns
of assumption, in the structures where they have long ago
become 'presumptuous'? I can doubtless damn myself by a
perverted mind. But how about the safety of the corporate
'thoughts' that are having the 'dominion' over the communities
of men? What might *sophrosyne* mean in a world bullied by
slogans and beset by tyrannous habits of the structures,
whether of tradition or of establishment, which ideas have
engineered?

'The sound mind' will need to be not only a mind of
thoughts safe inwardly to the person, crucial as these are. It
must mean for him also, as far as in him lies, 'a mind whose
thoughts are saving', outwardly in the fabric of the world. For
'safe' read 'saving' and do we not have the Christian
enlargement of the Greek ideal? 'The sound mind' in the
positive sense is the mind that wills to think redemptively in
every situation. Its thoughts intend salvation, deliberately and
hopefully. It is set, with due realism, for truth, for peace and
joy, for reconciliation. It is ready for the liabilities of its
intention, including those in which it is involved by men who
fear that salvation itself is an illusory or a pretentious word.

Such a mind is 'the mind of Christ' and the proper partner of
the 'power and love' with which it is linked in 2 Tim. 1.7. That
partnership surely confirms our Christian reading in the Greek
term. For power is hardly needed merely to admit frailty or
preserve a prudent modesty. Nor is love necessary only to
avoid excess or play safe in the stakes of life. But power and
love together are at a stretch to think redemption in all time
and place—power in that the task is unremitting and the
demands perpetual, love because saving thoughts must always

seek and find co-operation and community. It would be the final irony if 'presumption' overtook even our will to save.

There is one important element in what, in the light of the foregoing, we may perhaps call 'saving-mindedness'. It is that the doctrines and formulations of religion, or of faith, are not ends in themselves but, rather, instruments by which their meaning may become operative. Criteria of authority for those within them, they are presentations of meaning for those outside them. Though the inward authority serves their commendation, it does not warrant their significance. Truth offers credentials but waits for recognition. What matters, therefore, in the mediation of our faith to men is not, primarily, their assent to our *credo*, but their discovery of its worth, while the ultimate of our Christian duty is not to have our faith state itself like a theorem, but to fulfil itself like love. Where contradiction is clear, doctrine must not pretend there is identity. But, with the human bond unbroken, the point must be taken into activity and life, in hope and patience. As a credal formula, 'in Christ' will require us to exclude: but as an ambition and instinct no exclusions will be possible. We must always be finding the conciliatory area between ourselves and others and locating it in common action where that can be loyally prior to common conviction.

These are some of the assumptions of the saving mind. Trusting the Lord, as we do, *for* salvation, we must also trust him *with* it, allow, that is, that his purposes—believing as we must that we have the clue to them—nevertheless transcend, and maybe override, our care of them. *Accipe curam meam et tuam* is a familiar charge within the Church. Sometimes we forget to hear it from the Lord himself.

The saving mind looks always for partners, holds out for ends and cares for means. We can readily study its vocation under those three phrases. The Christian can understand himself, *vis-à-vis* other religion, as committed to relationships, bound by criteria, and ready for ministries, and each of these in the stress and moil of human affairs. Such is mission, deriving from the mission of God in Christ.

The seeking for partners is perhaps easier than it used to be, in physical and social terms, though it remains exacting otherwise. For one thing, other faiths are still liable to the sort of 'only us' which, to be truthful, has often characterised the Christian mind. Monopolies of mystery and meaning comfort and simplify. But we need to think and feel beyond them.

A striking example is to hand in the recent publication, *Islam and the Plight of Modern Man*, by the distinguished Persian philosopher and man of letters, Seyyed Hossein Nasr.[1] In part it echoes his earlier writings,[2] but its main purpose is to salute and interpret the 1976 World Festival of Islam in Britain. It explores the deep restlessness of technological man as the west manifests it, deplores the spread of that malaise into the contemporary Islamic world, and presents a strong esoteric, Sufi version of Islam as the effective analysis and remedy.

> Our concern is with the Truth . . . as the criterion of all human activity in either East or West in all times, past, present and future: it is with Islam as the last terrestrial expression of this Truth and as a living reality, a reality which can provide the necessary criteria to judge, according to permanent and immutable archetypes beyond the confines of space and time, the thoughts and actions of men. . . . [3]

The sensitive western reader readily kindles to the case being made. 'Modern man has forgotten who he is', he is 'devoid of a spiritual horizon'; 'he has become a prisoner to the pettiness of his own trivial creations and inventions'.[4] So far so good, though 'trivial' is, perhaps, a superficial word. Into this perilous loss of significance and direction comes the light of Islam.

What, however, surprises is the almost total neglect, or unawareness, of western spiritual travail in precisely the same diagnosis and urgency. The range and depth of World Council of Churches' thinking about the ecological problem, even the Stockholm Conference of 1972 of UNO, and the Papers and Agendas of successive WCC Assemblies are all ignored. The reader searches in vain for any penetration of western spirituality or alertness to its relevance in, e.g. Dag Hammarskjöld, de Chardin, Pasternak, William Temple, the

Niebuhr brothers, T. S. Eliot (one cursory reference), W. H. Auden and a host of others. Nor is there any attempt to register the intensity, and burden, of the search for meaning as we find it in Kafka, Camus, Golding and the rest, while, among older writers, Dostoevsky is dismissed as 'subjective'. All these are radical students, not to say explorers, of 'the plight of modern man', and their interrogation of life and religion is properly a field of attention for those who claim the answers.

The need to have man remember who he is is too pressing and, potentially, too unifying across our frontiers, to allow us to be deterred by this 'go-it-alone' stance from such an able and philosophical source. But it is worth reflecting on how it comes about that western spirituality, whether in existential questioning, or in Christian conviction, is so closed a book to a lively Muslim mind in an interpretative Islamic occasion. Were we closer together, we might both probe deeper and reach further: we might ponder whether our plight is what we have forgotten or how we have rebelled, whether the answer is recollection or redemption. But those issues require, in the first place, that we should be in genuine and open converse.

A very different aspect of the tasks involved in seeking partners is clear from the March 1976 conference in Tripoli, Libya, when some fifteen Roman Catholic theologians met a similar number of Muslim shaikhs (with some five-hundred guests in attendance, many of them journalists) at the invitation of the Libyan Government. Its Minister of Education, Dr M. A. Sharif, called upon the participants 'to work together in meeting the challenges of the age'. The Libyan leader, Colonel Qaddafi himself, interrogated the Christian theologians, asking whether there was one religion or many. If it is one, then by its guidance we can solve all questions. For that one religion has a blue-printed political economy and social order built on revelation, to follow which is not to err.

The one-that-is-right mentality has, of course, often pervaded the Christian's self-understanding with the Gospel. It is natural that it should, though the reasons differ from those which, variously, operate in other systems. Faith would not be faith anywhere if it indifferently identified all alternatives. Yet uniqueness, in itself, was never the credential of the Gospel and, properly understood, never could be. For it is only realised in the sequel to faith. What inspires and warrants us in going out to seek partnerships in the actual world with men of other creeds is not a syncretistic nonchalance about the differences but a positive confidence in the will and relevance of Christ. It is also that there are desperate tasks of compassion in society and urgent business about poverty, housing, exploitation and disease, which will not wait for the conclusions of abstract debate within theology. Examples, like the two above, of self-containedness in our neighbours, are more likely to be overcome and persuaded into conversation, if we, for our part, have an evident readiness for meeting, taking with us, in mutual respect, the credentials to which Christ binds us. Such ventures will mean no disloyalty. Rather, the disloyal thing will be to hold aloof.

In spite of what might deter us, whether from without or from within, through self-sufficiency—other men's or ours—numerous occasions of such active relating to each other present themselves. The saving mind has no lack of invitation to its calling. There are plenty of misadventures of ideas to rescue, implications to develop, possibilities to broach, wistfulnesses to satisfy, controversies to disentangle, not—it will be well to add—advantages to be taken. For where there are trust and integrity, there is no exploitation of the other, no cribbing to score points, no turning significant scepticism into actual witness, no reading between the lines what is not in them. Partnerships, moreover, have to be two-way. The Christian stands as much to gain from being freely catechised and criticised as he does from inquiring what others mean and hold. Not infrequently what others deplore or resist about him is what they have traditionally misread, and even when rejection remains substantial and is open-eyed it is to be preferred to apathy or misconception. We can allow ourselves here a few random examples of this kind of saving mind caring about other faiths and their societies, or about agnosticisms of any vintage. If, despite what has been said here, a mind to save is taken to be slanted, prejudicial, interested, and, therefore, incompatible with relationship, then we must either conclude that religions are inherently insulated from all interrelevance—which would mean despair, or else that our only option is the purely academic. Whatever may be true of archaeology, or geology, or metallurgy, religion is one area where academicism is sadly incomplete. Islam does not exist to be interesting, nor Buddhism for erudite discussion. Religions require religious reckoning, just as Christianity offers religious community. The posture of the saving mind is simply taking all faiths in their own seriousness, provided that the meaning of salvation remains itself a question.

Chapter 1 took its way into the business of living via the conversation of Arjuna and Krishna in the Bhagavad Gita, where the former's reluctance for the battle was overcome by the latter's call to unmotivated action. The warrior is to come through with his role-fidelity against the scruples of his personal feeling, his distaste for combat, his sense of futility. It is so fated, in that greater issues within karmic necessity turn upon such conformity than can be outweighed by personal dismay or individual conscience. The slain of the coming warfare are, so to speak, already dead. A society which is not motivated by *dharma*/duty will be inviting chaos. The evils which Arjuna fears and suspects are already neutralised by the will to disinterest in the midst of action. The vision of Lord Krishna seals and finalises the issue.

Mountaineers say they climb mountains because they are there. To do so in hope of a knighthood, a place in history, or lucrative reward, would somehow disqualify the climbing and spell disparagement of the mountain. This unmotivated dedication raises no problem: it has implicit admiration from all who understand its quality. But can we comprehend life and society in like terms? Is there not a sort of neutralism about a mountain which war, economy, society, history, scholarship, and the rest, do not possess? In these, and other, realms, 'be what you are' cannot be a static liability, since we and the other fellow are human, before we are artisan, or warrior, or scholar, and there is an obligation to relate roles to well-being in unceasing discrimination of responsibility. Unless we take refuge in its mystical climax of ecstatic vision, the Gita would seem to miss the dynamism which properly relates the personal to the social and the social to the moral and all these to the spiritual. The saving mind will certainly deal with motives; for there much of its task belongs. But it will not deal with them by the cult of disinterest, where disinterest is conformist to assumptions which themselves must be explored. Society, as Plato argued, is indeed well served if the cobbler is a good cobbler and does not masquerade as a surgeon. But that sort of prescript trusts human nature too much with too little.

How to purify intention has been a perpetual preoccupation of religion and a large dimension in salvation. 'Purity of heart', wrote Kierkegaard, 'is to will one thing'.[5] Life has a hundred conspiracies against the disinterestedness of true mountaineers. Is there, in the Gita, by Christian criteria, too naïve a stance, linked as we are in the central theme of motive? But what, in that sense, might seem too sanguine, is from another angle too negative of hope. The sense of karmic necessity which runs through Asian religion takes the past seriously as an entail and a sequence. Things done are irreversible: guilt has momentum: what has been conditions what is. No intelligent salvation can ignore these continuities. But given that relationality which pronounal faith confesses, forgiveness becomes a genuine possibility, a received experience. The prodigal son never ceases to be the son with the acquisitive past, the man once at the swine trough, in the bitter wretchedness of self-discovery. But, thanks to compassionate relationship, restoration happens and the very despair becomes the material of a personality remade. Retrospectively the sense of something forfeited ('I am no more worthy to be called your son') is a more radical sense of *karma* than *karma* itself, because it is open to genuine forgiveness. The saving dimension enters into the karmic, not by denying that entail is there, but by seeing it within a deeper context still, namely that of a cosmic element of love which can halt and reverse it. That context, however, brings us back into the language, and the confidence, of pronounal faith. If necessitarians about the past, in Asian religion, can bring themselves to see that forgiven state, their sense of things is not ignored. It is present in the very nature of forgiveness, but without despair, very much as weight is present in the strength of the arch. Its meaning is there as part of the secret of the thing which overcomes it.

Is there not a comparable situation when we think savingly about that human impermanence which lay so close to the springs of Buddhism? Sickness, decrepitude and death—these were the burdens of the Buddha's search for truth. They seemed to say: 'You cannot find it here.' Hence the desire to repudiate desire as that which perpetuates the hopeless state of man in the body. Hence, too, the urge to that compassion which, in Buddhism, has so nobly cared for the pathos of the human. Here are themes very close to salvation, if the diagnosis is acceptable.

But does life's movement deathwards admit only of this interpretation? Procreation, as we noted in the Qur'an, persists. Youth is renewed and through the generations truth endures. If life is a subtraction of days until we reach a zero of demise, it is also an addition sum by which occasions ripen and significance matures. Need we conclude that what has a limit thereby has futility? Content and duration are not identical accounts of time. There is an intriguing ambiguity in the very word 'end' which suggests that purpose and terminus, destiny and fleetingness, are not necessarily exclusive of each other. At least the option must remain that we judge from content, rather than from transitoriness, in deciding about life, and ask, with Browning, of hope and meaning: 'Has it your vote to be so if it can?'[6]

But these, it will be said, are saving thoughts at their crudest, since Buddhism is more subtle than these reflections understand. There is a more inclusive detachment from the historical than mere pessimism about mortality and death. Agreed. The compassion of the Buddha, of the *Bodhisattvas*, the saviours who defer *Nirvana* in order to aid the souls of men, has a deeper goal. The samsaric flux is itself, we might almost say, to be *Nirvana*, in being lived detachedly, in being taken, as it were, beyond the illusions of desire even in its very incidence. Yet will compassion, so practised and so conceived, adequately relate to a situation in which there is not merely flux but distinction, not only transience but evil? Must not the way to peace somehow grapple with the Napoleons, the Eichmanns, the Watergates of this world and with their lieutenants within us all? May not this mean that the very samsaric realities, as Buddhists see them, require something like the Cross-peace which Christians identify in Christ—a peace which has the full measure of Buddhist, human pathos but also of actual, human moral evil, a peace which has borne the wrong as well as interpreted the yearning?

There is a wistful poem of the poet F. Tyutchev, which, aside from its characteristic Russian land-love, seems to capture vividly that elemental human condition of which, in different idiom, the Asian faiths are so firmly conscious.

> These poor hamlets, humbling faring,
> Nature sunk in desolation,
> Land of mine such sorrows bearing,
> Land of all the Russian nation.
>
> Nothing knowing, nothing seeing,
> How can haughty foreign faces
> Mark what mystery has being
> In the lowly naked places?

That pathos, and the supercilious unawareness which cannot read it, might roughly tally with the Asian reading and the western ignorance. But Tyutchev continues:

> There was One, my land, who knew thee
> With a Cross upon Him pressing,
> Like a servant walking through thee,
> Heaven's King bestowed His blessing.[7]

There is the Christian case, in its simplicity—a compassion, understood as transcendent in origin and quality, interpreting and saving the human condition by the grace of a love that suffers. To identify such a presence one is not far from the heart of Buddhist pathos but with another response.

It is 'other' because it involves those pronouns where so much turned in Chapter 3. They seem to be clues at every turn. For they are present, seriously, again when we try, as outsiders, to assess the question of the self in Theravada or Hinayana Buddhism. Is the selflessness there sought a metaphysical or a moral quest? It certainly means to be the former. But does experience seem to suggest that it can only be the latter? In the Theravada tradition there is a strong emphasis on 'Work out your own salvation', a rigorous discipline which makes it essentially a monk's task with 'little to offer the layman beyond the conventional homilies'.[8] Can we liken the problem to the one which Luther faced, namely that every effort to escape the self in personal discipline and abnegation only left one more desperately with the self? Did this, further, imply that selflessness could be blessedly an ethical goal, but one would always need the self to reach it?

It was, in part, to meet the problem of the Theravada monk striving to unself himself that the whole Mahayana tradition developed, with its greater openness to the lay world and its accent on 'means of grace' and aid, in a word, its more religious, as distinct from moral, resources. Yet still the problem of 'me' and 'mine' persists. How do we shed this delusive selfhood, since shedding it is the clue to salvation? Desire has somehow to be the *tanha*, or thrust, within its own negation. It may be crude to ask the Buddhist who or what is it that enters *Nirvana*. For the question betrays a remoteness from the meaning, like asking whether Pilate is not really to be credited with the salvation of the world since his decision was necessary to the Cross of Jesus happening. But desire is still there within the will to end it. May this not require us to conclude that it is, in fact, ineluctable?

Saving thoughts, then, looking for relationship and holding to clues, will go far with the Buddhist sense of things. For the self, truly, has no enemy worse than itself. Desire is the crux. But, as indeed within Buddhism, it has to be recruited for its own saving not, as in Stoicism, by a sustained sulkiness meant to double-cross the risks of life by not incurring them, nor yet in the nobler sense of the Buddhist as invited into undesiring. For even the abeyance of will must be willed, and sustained. Does this paradox lead us, like Paul's schoolmaster, toward Christ, in that the desiring self desires unselfishly?

There are themes of a very different order when Islam is concerned. Two related questions can perhaps illuminate and do duty for the rest. They have to do with God's sovereignty and man's response and with the divine mercy. It would seem that not all Muslims recognise the implications of the fact of idolatry which is central to the genesis and the abiding significance of their faith. Islam, from the beginning, has been set for the elimination of idolatry. Muhammad's mission denounced *shirk* and positively affirmed the sole worship, the absolute oneness, of God. 'Truly *shirk* is great wrong', says Surah 31.13. The term means any diversion of faith, trust, reliance, worship, hope and fear, properly due, as these are, to God, to any pseudo-deity. *Shirk* is the antonym to *islām*. It is the antithesis of the primary obligation of the Muslim to worship only God in undeviating loyalty. His creed, or *shahādah*, negates all idols. 'There is no god except God'—the necessary form of true faith in a society given to plural worship. To repudiate the idols was the central passion of the Prophet's mission: to educate mankind into liberating acknowledgement of the divine unity was the great purpose of the Quranic revelation: to confirm and enforce it is the function of Islamic polity.

What large and emancipating implications are here! A true worship is very close to the Christian meaning of salvation. 'Let God be God' is the common cry between us. But have we fully taken the meaning of the fact that idolatry occurs at all and that it can be so endemic as to need so emphatic a revelatory repudiation? God, it is clear—the God of Islam and of Christianity—is one we humans may ignore and defy to the length of substituting for his power and wisdom the false worships of our fantasy and our rebellion. He has, then, the magnanimity to make and leave us free. Given the actuality of idolatry, we cannot interpret his omnipotence as so distrustful of its competence as to withhold from the creature man the freedom even to deny him. The possibility, and the fact, of idolatry mean that the only other option is a *willing* worship.

It is important to appreciate what this means for our notions of omnipotence for it is precisely there that the saving Christian mind has so much business with the Muslim. All too often one meets the crude notion that omnipotence means the divine ability to do anything, that divine lordship must be seen as incapable even of self-limitation, that the divine is never to be thought of as other than utterly unconstrained. Yet idolatry happens. We cannot conclude some divine indifference to it—certainly not in the light of urgent revelation to denounce it. Plainly *shirk* must matter to God: yet men are free to perpetrate it. It seems clear that the divine will to a true worship is not irresistible. The more we are tempted to think that the omnipotent is the irresistible the less omnipotent in any real or Muslim sense it becomes. As expressed in the creation, and the creature man, God's omnipotence is *not* an ability to do anything. If we are to make sense of the faith in creation we and Muslims possess, omnipotence must mean the competence whereby God's sovereignty prevails within the actualities, the risks we might almost say, which creation involves, including that human liberty to make idols. A humanity which needs the prophets, calling it into *islām*, is manifestly under an omnipotence that works, not in arbitrary dictatorship, but through the educated autonomy of man. 'He will not have us accept His purposes save as our own.'[9]

This Islamic/Christian reading of a theology of man reaches significantly into the contemporary situation. Idolatry is no ancient and antiquated evil, occurring in primitive societies lost in *Jahiliyyah* (as the Muslim term is), sunk in ignorance and non-revelation. It takes sophisticated form wherever men absolutise their structures of power and the divine lordship is decried or ignored in pride or indifference. Those subtle idols may be race, or nation, or science, or technology, or party, or profit. The meaning of 'Let God be God' is to relativise all else, to find in a true worship that which alone obviates and subdues all false ones.

The pseudo-absolutes would not arise unless they were legitimate—as relative. The restlessness man experiences in giving them a total worship is the nemesis their falsehood brings upon him. It is also the proof that he is meant for God, under whose acknowledged authority they will be rescued from the absoluteness which makes them idolatrous and tyrannical and saved for the ends they properly fill within the human scene. It is thus judging them that the active mystery of the divine lordship is known for what it is.[10]

But still it remains uncompulsive. Man the idolater has to

become man the submitter, the complier with truth, the *muslim* (as the technical Muslim term is). He will not be saved against himself. The Christian faith, from the New Testament onwards, has shared, after its own manner, this insistent 'keep yourselves from idols' (1 John 5.21)—to quote perhaps the last New Testament words to be penned.[11] But, important as it is to make this point of a common front against idolatry, the ultimate question is the pattern of the divine and human conquest of it. Divine and human, of course, it has to be. For the evil only exists in a human flouting of the divine. It must deal uncompulsively with the impulses by which man (we must coin the word) idolatrises. For if it were to be a compulsive solution, why not compulsively prevent the problem in the first place, or have solved it by *diktat* long ago? Moreover, as the Qur'an itself declares: 'There is no compulsion in religion' (2.256).

Islam, here, understands the divine will as relying on revelation, education, habituation, and exhortation. The availability of all these in the Scripture, the *Din* or religion, the *Shari'ah* or Law, represent the mercy of God, celebrated so faithfully in *Bismillah*, or invocation of 'the merciful Lord of mercy'. That mercy, operating through these institutions of religion, warrants Islamic confidence in the perfectibility of man and the feasibility of the due obedience. The idols whose worship arises from credulity, or ignorance, or frailty, or weakness, will be defeated by knowledge, and that concert of a single worship which Islam accomplishes. In and around and beyond all is the divine mercy.

A saving Christian thought here takes further the clue of a divine vulnerability already discerned in the fact of idolatry at all. There cannot be significant idolatry and divine immunity. What makes man an idolater, ancient or modern, is a perversity more than a forgetfulness, a self-love more than a frailty. On the divine side too, the rejection implicit in idolatry deepens into brutality to prophet-messengers calling to true worship and finally into that central compassionate encounter of the divine will to be loved and the human will to defy which we have studied in Chapter 4, where the divine mercy saves us from ourselves, and so grounds a true worship in the autonomy of human love.

If these paragraphs avail, in any sense, to illustrate how saving thoughts might mediate between religions, not asking their submission or proposing their displacement, but exploring their human and their transcendental content, the sceptic may still see them as no more than an exercise in Christian prejudice. If so, realism and honesty can leave him behind. Some scepticisms, admittedly, are invincible. The saving mind, anyway, is not a pedestrian on a one-way street. Its affirmatives are also interrogatives, its commendations open to interrogation. But realism must be reciprocal, offered and received.

Where, it may be asked in all this, is the place of the secular? How does the saving mind relate to the temper that finds salvation ludicrous, naïve, or pretentious? Or to the instinct which, if there is salvation at all, throws us back upon our own human resources and the values for which we struggle, amid the intractables of politics and the economic, social order? If, as in these chapters, we are primarily concerned with the Christian and other religion, we will be relating to society through the religion that conditions it historically. But Chapter 1 assumed that there was more to religion than religions and alert secularism must certainly occupy the saving mind.

Much obtains here as in the relationship of historic and established faiths. There is a quality in radical, secular literature which is in fact already exploring questions to which religion offers answers. We must allow it to probe those answers unreservedly and willingly forego the notion that establishment means any monopoly of spirituality. Even some rugged and desperate intimation of the void may search the interpretation which has claimed to fill it. The Christian belief in the divine relevance to man is the better for an open reckoning with Samuel Beckett's communication of the unanswering mystery of popular theological imagination. To hold with a divine forgiveness really breaking the entail of our self-esteem is the wiser and the humbler for grappling with Camus who finds it altogether elusive and unreal.

At a different level are the sociologists and psychologists

who comprise the world we comprehend in terms that call for saving, as fit rather for description only, for analysis and report, as fundamentally value-free, where the most we can know of liberty is the extent of our imprisonment, where a plausibility-context determines all our knowing and believing, and to know it so is the measure of our realism and our emancipation.

There is perhaps little the saving mind can do to retrieve this situation since that mind itself is only evidence of a forlorn enterprise which has no capacity to gain the attention, still less the persuasion, of the realists. As with Freud's famous *Introductory Lectures*, any resistance to the diagnosis is only proof of the extent of the delusion. Religious salvationists are all too likely to be dismissed as the more evidence of their wishful state of mind.

But not always. The best hope is when the social scientific interpretation of the human situation incurs a mood of wistfulness and thinks further into its own sufficiencies, whether caught, momentarily, by Browning's 'grand perhaps', or yielding like Wittgenstein to the fascination of the mystics, or given pause by some 'rumour of angels', waiting on the wing. When this humility supervenes, there is much for all of us to learn on either side the fence of faith.

Peter Berger's *A Rumour of Angels* is just such a sample of occasion. His other works[12] are a somewhat bleak survey of sociological conditioning, for which society is value-free, and beliefs are not held *per se* for their worth or truth or meaning, but by dint of the plausibility-context which society engenders. But, in a mood of diffidence about this all-embracing sociology of faith, he wonders about possible 'signals from transcendence' which might be registered by man, not, of course, deduced or codified from historical experience, after the pattern of religious claims, but deducible from immediate data within the purview of the spirit of man. He finds them, for his part, in that experience of trust and being trusted which happens in the parent/child world; in play and games as giving us an angle on ourselves beyond ourselves; in humour where the comic somehow liberates us from the prison of the world; in the dimension of what a religious theology would call 'blasphemy', the sense of things which just ought not to be because the whole spirit cries out against their travesty of life; and, finally, in the dimension of hope by which man transcends where he is in a sense of where, or how, he might be. All these are 'divine signals in reality'.

Religion as vindicating laughter, the feeling that 'the denial of metaphysics (in secularisation) means the triumph of triviality',[13] any intelligent theologian would be overjoyed to accept as a *confessio fidei* from such a source, without pressing for a greater orthodoxy. Have we not always been saying, perhaps ineptly, that there were certain deeds that cry out to heaven, that there is what William Temple called 'the dreadful astonishment of God';[14] that joy is an index to hope and both an ally of the divine; that the kingdom of heaven has a likeness of the child and that procreative love and the ordering care of the home are due similes of an over-arching heaven.[15] But let us not be too proprietorial of these convictions or surprised because they have currency in unlikely quarters. It is rather the shame of our crudity or our unimaginative ways that it does not happen more widely. For all the clues are there in the human situation as it is. And such awarenesses, springing up anywhere, are just what we have always said we meant by the Holy Spirit, Lord and giver of life. Can we not properly leave all our saving thinking *vis-à-vis* the secular world in steady but energetic partnership, as much as in us lies, with the rumouring angels? William Blake thought they were in his garden and might be met in the Strand.

In all the foregoing, the aim has been to seek relationships and to hold criteria in Christ. It may be claimed that we have found the one and kept the other, seeing religious meeting in every direction, not as immediate recruitment to belief, but as mediation of meaning and understanding. But our third concern was to be caring for means. Is there not a practical commitment of the Christian community to co-operation in action as far as may be, political and social and personal, for the care of human problems and adversities? Whenever those problems take us, as they often do, into the abstracts of doctrine and culture, they are already in mind in the sample issues just reviewed. But, beyond the bearing of dogmas and

patterns of thought, are the situations themselves, whether
poverty, population, malnutrition, freedom, race, exploitation,
education, and the rest. The Christian relation with other
religion in all these areas is one of participation, in ministry
and in comprehension of their nature, as well as a deep
conscience for their burden on the human condition.

But everything that can be said, whether about service in the
concrete or thinking in the actual, presupposes Christians. It
may surprise some readers that thus far in our discussion,
aside from incidental references in Chapter 5 about C. F.
Andrews, nothing has been said about conversion. This has
been deliberate. It would be easy to summarise the whole
Christian relation to other religion simply by the word
evangelism, meaning by it the recruitment of souls into the
fold. Instead it has been left to the sphere of caring for means.
Plainly the surest means to Christian faith is the Christian
person. Everything in the end turns upon discipleship. But, if
discipleship is understood only as assent to a faith in its items,
rather than in its quality, and if the antecedent faith is seen
only as discarded, will the discipleship itself avail?

C. F. Andrews, responding to Gandhi's demand for a
complete repudiation of the will to convert, insisted that no
Christian could ever properly agree. A static notion of once-
born believing has no place in the dynamism of Christianity.
The Gospel is committed to what we might call the
convertibility of man. If the faith could only be had by birth it
would deny its own most precious quality—its openness to all
mankind. It must always be in a posture of saying to the world:
'That you also may have fellowship with us . . .' (1 John 1.3).
For otherwise it becomes an inaccessible perquisite of the
accident of place or race or family and, as such, would have
betrayed itself.

It is also true that baptism of the person has been the
historic mark of the access to the Christian community, and is
included in the Gospel versions of the great commission. The
faith does not exist to be patronised or merely pondered. Christ
is not for gestures of interest, but for surrenders of heart.

Yet the evangelical 'making of disciples' by 'going into all
the world' is much more than the recruiting sergeant on the

beat. Discipleship is a ripe and strenuous thing. We have lost much by thinking of the world of our commission as simply geographical, or of mission as essentially a matter of journeys. 'The world' is, more properly, just that taxing, puzzling, daunting, inviting territory of religious and other cultures and communities, which we do not penetrate if we have first excluded them from our entering. 'Christ' said Paul, 'sent me not to baptise but to preach' (1 Cor. 1.17). His meaning is not immediately plain and it is clearly not an absolute negation. But it seems to assert a priority for penetration of meaning over accession of people.

People, moreover, are not themselves in total detachment from what they have been. 'How can a man be born when he is old?' was, on the part of Nicodemus (John 3.4), a very sensible question. The point was that he did not understand the new birth of which Jesus spoke. There is, indeed, no entering of the womb again to jettison and replace all that makes a person, beginning with the embryonic mystery, via the mother's milk, and maturing into a language, a landscape, a culture, a family, a fabric of living, all of them quite irreversible. Into these 'givens' of our making comes the spiritual regeneration which does not terminate what we are by identity but, rather, saves it in the newness of life. In all those determinants which abide, religion plays its part and will accordingly persist in the new that is in Christ, radically renewed to be sure, but not abrogated in the personal equation. Even conversion itself, then, when we come to it, has to relate to the cultural relevance and the spiritual meanings of the faith within which the Holy Spirit brings it.

But, given such due reverence and perspective, there can be no doubt that Christians are the final asset, the ultimate determinant, of the faith of Christ. The saving mind cannot walk around except in persons. The whole logic of all the foregoing is the nurture, the enlargement, of the Christian community, not self-centredly, but as the earthen vessels for the treasure. Reverence for reverence, everywhere, must include discipleship to discipleship. All dialogue with faiths presupposes commitment in faith. The sort of saving thoughts studied in this chapter mean the steady pastoral nurture of the

Christian within the Church. We cannot be taking other religion in its seriousness if we fail to recognise the seriousness of the Gospel. To do this is to know that 'Whosoever will may come'. The surest means to the meanings of the faith is the mind that perceives them, the heart that loves them and the will that serves them. The partnerships of the Holy Spirit have always been with people.

That conviction, surely biblical enough, leaves one final question. It is a question which bears closely on relations with Judaism. Here the business of the saving mind is uniquely at a stretch, so much in love and debt, so much in hope and contrast. Jewry, as we noted in Chapter 2, broadly speaking, sees a Messiahship actual in history as a contradiction. To have the fact is not to have the hope. Moreover, though Christianity may in some sense be valid for Gentiles (as a way of *their* participation in the mystery of God's grace), Israel must always exempt itself from that alleged fulfilment of its deepest theme. This loyalty to the Torah covenant involves a sharp issue about the very feasibility of the Church as the universal form of divine servanthood in the world. For such universality cannot be squared with the Judaic sense of

> ... the history of creation, which develops into the history, not of the nations but of Israel: second, the revelation of God ... and third, the messianic prophecy, whose centre and focal point is the effort of the people of Israel for the redemption of humanity.[16]

What is at stake here is our very authenticity in the will to be 'church'. For the Church, in the New Testament, believing, by its Jewish tutelage, in peoplehood, nevertheless sees that community fellowship as no longer ethnic, no longer private, no longer based on land and nation, but open on the sole ground of faith to all mankind. Buber even protests that this transcendence by the church of blood and soil and nation 'desanctifies' these 'elemental forces' of the world.[17] There is for him either a naïveté, or an illusion, in the notion that divine peoplehood in divine purpose could obtain in the open terms the Church, in New Testament understanding, is believed to constitute.

This deep contention over the church-form of being 'people of God', and the sense of Jesus' Messiahship from which it emerges, together present the Christian mind with wide occasions of relationship. God's presence in history is less definitive for Jewry than for Christians,[18] but the service of that presence is more intimate. Without the Incarnation, the Judaic faith is proud to trust 'the light of the countenance' (Num. 6.25–7), not in the Son of Man crucified but, all such image apart, in the fidelity of their people's covenant. Contrariwise, the Christian Church, finding 'the light of the knowledge of the glory of God in the face of Jesus Christ' (2 Cor. 4.6), takes its vocation into the wideness of the world both for acceptance and recruitment.

There are, here, kinships of faith across tensions of contrast and these impossible to isolate from centuries of tragic history. May it be that the hope we believe to be realised in Christ according to Jesus is the pattern of the hope they still await, and that their fidelity of vocation remains the measure of the calling we have presumed to universalise?

7 The Holy Spirit

'CAN'T you stick on somepin from Scripture so it'll be religious?' In John Steinbeck's *The Grapes of Wrath* old grandpa has died at the roadside on the trek west. The family decides to bury him themselves, being in no position to bear the cost, or the ceremony, of a funeral. But, fearing suspicion from the authorities over such a covert act, they bury with the corpse a simple statement, sealed in a jam-jar, stating the facts as they were: 'This here is Wm. Joad, died of a stroke, old, old man: his fokes bured him becaws they got no money to pay for funerals.'[1]

The suggestion about the text to round off the document is something of an afterthought. Casey, the derelict ex-preacher, trekking with the family, is the obvious candidate for the task of choosing one. Being who he is, the Bible is his natural quarry and verses aplenty are to hand, about the Lord and the shepherd, not to mention being 'Safe in the arms of Jesus'.

All this is a long way from our sophisticated themes in these pages. Or is it? At least, the phrase is a haunting one: 'So it'll be religious.' What, exactly, does that adjective describe? What, it is fair to ask, does the text add to the words of fact? Why should it be wanted? The 'religiousness' is already there—in the mortal pathos, in the dumb tragedy of social wrongs stoically borne, in the dignity of human courage in lowly quarters, in reverence for the dead, in the will to come clean, in the integrity that anticipates and cares about justification, in the family unity, in the patience of grief. With these, has the psalmist or the evangelist anything more to say?

Yet would the Joads have been this sort of people had they not also been the sort to want a text? Perhaps, in a way, the significance of the text is there already in the quality of their soul, in the texture of their character. Writing it in as an appendix simply seals what is, and does not make it so. Were that something otherwise, no quotation-mongering could save it. Wanting the verse, we have to conclude, like wanting a kiss or an embrace, does not import the extraneous. It expresses the inward. We might almost make the paradox that if the Joads had not wanted the text it would not have been necessary.

This incident may seem a curious start to reflections on the Holy Spirit. But precisely 'being religious' is what all the foregoing is about, however debatable, inadequate or, to many, provocative, that phrase may be. Wherever people, in funerals or festivals, in coming and going, in living and dying, in grieving and celebrating, in soul and in symbol, are 'being religious', it would seem that we find three elements in the whole. It is around these that our study in the Holy Spirit must revolve. They are the impulse, the reasoning and the shape. There is the prompting that initiates, the conceiving that actuates and the expressing which associates or devises, out of its partners, the deed, the symbol, the art, the pattern, without which motive and mind have, so to speak, no form. From Abraham to Solzhenitzin, shall we say, these, in their ripe or uneasy relation, are as with the Joads in their migration, the stuff of the sacred, the nature of religion.

So it will be right to think of the Holy Spirit, in the work of the saving mind, just outlined, as being there where men will, and think, and do, within their systems and their lights. Prompting is personal, social, economic, political, creative and artistic. Conceiving is philosophical, mental, theological, scientific, ideological and imaginative. Expressing is active, cultural, institutional, liturgical, symbolic, physical, literary and spiritual. The Christian, relating to other religion in all these areas of their life and character, prays and hopes to be the means of the Holy Spirit's presence and grace, his truth and hope and patience.

Before considering some aspects of this calling there are three general questions we need to review. The first has to do with the faith we may have in the activity of the Holy Spirit beyond the Scriptures and the Church. This question, of course, was implicit in the exclusive/inclusive issues which, in

Chapter 5, we centred upon Christ and the Gospel. Some would insist with Hippolytus: 'I believe in the Holy Spirit in the Holy Church.'[2] The Fourth Gospel insistently conjoins the Spirit with what we have earlier called the Christic. 'I will come to you' and 'When the Spirit of truth is come' suggest the once-for-all historical and the here-and-now perpetual as belonging definitively together. 'He shall take of mine', 'He shall not speak from himself'. Whether the famous *Filioque* should read 'and the Son' or 'through the Son' is not here relevant to the 'proceeding'. That fascinating (now much depreciated) word certainly means a continuum of energy and meaning whereby the Father is known in the Son and they are active, self-consistently, through the Spirit. That New Testament emphasis should give us pause in assuming we might set such continuity aside.[3] God in the Spirit, according to the Gospels, is God in Christ. We might translate the verb 'proceeding' as truth in its own energies, in channels of its own making, like the dialectic of a loving reason. It is not a word which rides readily with things haphazard, or with vagaries of mind. If, in St John's concern, there were gnostics emasculating or evacuating the redeeming history, have we no cause to be wary of their contemporary counterparts?

Nevertheless, the wind blows where it lists. It would not be well to think Christ's significance to be subject to monopoly possession. While 'the cistern contains', as William Blake observed, 'the fountain overflows',[4] and 'to overflow' is very much the sense of the verb in John 15.26. Theology has so often, to its loss, preferred the cistern. The Spirit's taking and opening of the things of Christ, true to the pattern of the definitive Messiahship, has place for the unexpected and the disconcerting. This must be so, if only because our own Christian reception of the faith may have unwittingly abandoned or conveniently ignored something of its range. Or it may be so again because the mind of the time is not attuned to the credentials that Christian custodians of Christ have to offer it. There are those, for example, who imagine that to believe is to have no more interrogatives and, being unable to surrender these, have no will to heed such witnesses. Or, yet again, as in the breadth of Asia, it may be that thoughts turn to

Christ without the background of Old Testament ideas of God—thoughts which, therefore, need to reckon with the Incarnation, not within the Jewish vision of God, but within *brahmavidya* concepts of supreme union with the absolute and the tangle of those concepts with puranic ideas of many *avatars*. Such a reckoning with the Christic meaning will be very much a school of Christian faith, but far outside the prescripts of New Testament vocabulary and shape of mind.[5] Some, perhaps, may wonder whether such a context admits of being phrased in terms of 'proceeding from the Father and the Son'. But can it be not so, if he is indeed 'the Saviour of the world'? The ways of the Spirit cannot be exclusive of the life and mystery of other faiths unless we are to surrender a Christ for the world. It is precisely the partiality of all human witness that necessitates the universal witness of the Spirit and necessitates, too, the genuine partnership between them.

'Christianity', remarked a friend of Klaus Klostermaier, 'is underdeveloped.'[6] A humbling idea, after these two thousand years. Yet it might be understood consistently with the word of Jesus, according to John, about the 'many things to say' which then they could not bear, and the pledge, in that very context, of 'the Spirit of truth to guide . . . into all truth' (John 16.12–13), if, that is, we can include the centuries in the community of the discipleship, and the lands as well. But then, if we cannot so include them, we are left either with an archaic faith or a static one. In either case the Holy Spirit, far from 'proceeding', is, in brutal language, either redundant or unemployed. So then, the very finality of the Gospel of Christ argues the unceasing and unfailing Spirit of God everywhere at work.

Our second consideration has to do with the relation of spirit and form—a perennial issue when meaning and institution come together, as come together they must in the life of society. If one speaks, in the language of 1 Tim. 3.15, of 'the church of the living God, the pillar and the ground of truth', in what sense can one set the word 'is' between those two clauses? That 'the church *is* the ground of truth' is clearly what the writer is intending to say and that 'church' is a place where Timothy 'behaves', which he serves, to which he belongs. As both community and in some sense structure and society, it is an entity, an institution, a fact. Yet the definition, or the predicate here made about it, does not automatically happen because it exists. What it *is*, as it were, in identity, it has to be in actuality. Its being, we may say, is in becoming, and its becoming is the realisation of its being. Between these two every kind of misconception, false confidence, frustration, and, happily, achievement and opportunity, may arise.

An immediate illustration is to hand in the nature of Christian marriage. It *is*, we say, indissoluble. But that principle, arbitrarily imposed, does not fulfil itself in fact. Understood as the place for a steady achievement of mutuality, fulfilment can happen, but only creatively, when the concept is taken as the structure of vocation. Christian marriage 'makes' wife and husband and then says to them: 'Be what you are.' But that being is perpetual attainment, aided, truly, by the mystery of the status conferred, but not, by that status, just occurring. Wedlock may be deadlock: which is to say, not that abidingness is wrong but that institutionalising it will not, of itself, ensure it. Yet the institution is the form through which love wills to unite, in that utter quality which love truly spells and makes.

John Milton had the situation, feelingly, in his *Doctrine and Discipline of Divorce*:

> ... in the blessing of matrimony not seldom [changed] into a familiar and co-inhabiting mischief: at least into a drooping and disconsolate household captivity, without refuge or redemption ... to fadge together and combine as they may to their unspeakable weariness and despair of all sociable delight in the very ordinance which God established to that end. What a calamity is here![7]

The true constancy of marriage is thus betrayed if union becomes inertia, or worse, rather than fidelity and kindling surprise. *These* are the indissolubility the form exists to structure. But structure, making for a status, is not the reality except it enables and houses the discipline and the devotion which are the active mystery of marriage.

This dilemma arising from the dependence of spirit on the instrument of form is familiar enough in many spheres. Here we apply it to the is-ness of the Church, of mission, of dogma, of the Christian thing, in their external forms. All these, like holy wedlock, can only be what they are in their committedness as they become what they must. The Holy Spirit is never imprisoned in the verb 'to be', as it relates to them. There are no automatic guarantees in the Holy Spirit, no established creeds, codes, churches, symbols, which avail and achieve just by dint of being there, of being right in form, of holding fast and keeping going. All these forms turn unceasingly for their virtue on the vitality of the Spirit of life and love and power. But spirituality does not, therefore, escape into formlessness. Every renewal of vitality faces anew the temptations of the old. The initiatives of the spirit and the liabilities of form can never be divorced and, for that reason, identity is never immune from ambiguity—or worse. All Christian relating to other religion is deeply involved here. There is no caring for spirituality that can ignore structures.

There is a third reflection, proper here, about the Holy Spirit at work in the breadth of the world and in the forms of religion. It takes us to what might be called movement into the present. Chapter 1 aimed to make our study duly contemporary, in alertness to where we are and to times in flux. But that is not only a matter of being alive to events and changing climates of mind. It is also a right sense of what the recent Report by the Doctrine Commission of the Church of England calls 'the pastness of the past'.[8] If, as we noted above in reference to the place-inclusiveness of the Spirit, the Christian faith is neither archaic nor static, then it must move with what may be called the time-inclusiveness of the Spirit.

> Divergencies in the way belief is expressed conceptually are to be expected from the very nature of Christian truth itself, and have in fact characterised the Church from New Testament times onwards.[9]

Because time, language, vocabulary, immediacies of life, are all in flux, it happens that defensive postures of faith, taken wisely in the past, have become no longer crucial or even intelligible. Contrariwise, in other directions, theology needs a fresh alertness truly to serve the threefold vocation studied in

Chapter 6. This, rightly disciplined, is not a question of syncretism, nor of disloyalty. Nor are these, except for the fearful, terms that should inhibit responsible fidelity. There must always be a balance between a theology which steadfastly sees all times within the framework of the one decisive event and a theology which lives that decisiveness within the present times. A Christian doctrine of the Holy Spirit certainly means that we 'go to school with the past',[10] learning at the Christ-crux of history, but that we go in the full consciousness of our generation.

Is it fair to comment, parenthetically, that we are in need of taking the issue of other religion into the concerns of the Doctrine Commission? Its Report might, arguably, be open to the sort of criticism brought in Chapter 6 to Dr S. H. Nasr's *Islam and the Plight of Modern Man*, namely that its stance is wholly within the single faith, except, of course, that *Christian Believing* relates to inward Christian themes and does not purport to be in the 'Christianity and...' concern. All its contributors, however, are in what might be called the domestics of Christian theology, while the practitioners on the borders so urgently need their Christian competence and expertise.

The Report ends its review with these words:

> ... the creeds as the classic formularies of Christendom ... will continue to be one of the major resources of God's people, inspiring each of us to go on from our individual starting-point and to take no rest, intellectually, spiritually, or morally, in the adventure of our journey into communion with the Love at the heart of all things.[11]

Our creeds and that human journey are what we have to hold together as Christians, and hold together among those, also, who would not yet, or ever, speak of 'God's people' or 'communion with the Love at the heart of things'. Faith in the Holy Spirit is the only conceivable capacity for such an enterprise.

To return to the Joads, are not the creeds among Christians in some sense the text written on our human mortality, our living–dying, 'so that it will be religious'? Having considered three basic issues—the Spirit 'proceeding', spirit and form and the Spirit and time, the rest of this concluding chapter takes in reverse order the triple themes discerned in that simple incident of grandpa's burial as Steinbeck has it. They were the impulse, the reasoning and the expression, or, more directly, the will, the thought and the deed. In the opposite order, for purposes of exposition, these become, in the larger context of Christian religiousness relating to the world under the Holy Spirit, the Christ-symbol, the divine logic and the will in Christ. Each of these dimensions of our mission moves with that commitment to relationships, pledgedness to criteria and readiness for ministry which were the themes of Chapter 6.

But first, that lingering distaste for the denominator 'religious', which we have acquired from Barth, Van Leeuwen, Bonhoeffer, Harvey Cox and a score of others.[12] Is 'religionising' life and the world in any conceivable sense the business of the Christian faith and Church?

It depends what we mean. There is point to religionlessness if the religion concerned relates to deities demised, or to pietisms unworthy, or to ecclesiasticisms falsely sacrosanct. But, rightly disowning these is not irreligion. On the contrary. If by religionlessness we intend escape from forms, the intention is illusory. Forms are inescapable: what matters is that they should be authentic. Charles Kingsley had the 'opiate of the people' diagnosis, in an Anglican rectory, before Marx hit upon it in the British Museum. Isaiah, of course, had it earlier still: 'Bring no more vain oblations . . . cease to do evil, learn to do well . . .' (Isa. 1.13,16,17). Faith is not unaware of the treachery of the pseudo-faithful. *Corruptio optimi pessima.* It is no wonder if liability for ultimacy should be most tempted to enormity, or that they 'who serve the greater cause may make the cause serve them'.[13]

'So that it'll be religious' means tying the part to the whole. It means refusing to absolutise the relative. It means allowing that the transcendent transcends. It means that man is more than scientific, more than political, more than animal, more than sexual, more than revolutionary, more than psychoanalysable, more than sociologically conditioned, more than technician. He is, to be sure, all these: but they do not exhaust him. The religious dimension is not another 'relative' (though its institutions will be), like the scientific, the aesthetic, or the artistic. Rather it is inclusive of all these, as that which gives them authenticity. Religion is the capacity to say Yes to mystery, to wonder, to curiosity, to hope; to say No to travesty, to futility, to cynicism. It is the ability to recognise blasphemy for what it is, to let awe and reverence prevail over the merely exploitative, possessive, or vulgarising instincts of human greed or pride. It is the ability for a numinous humility, a radical worship, an open wonder, a gentle wistfulness. It is the responsibility in inclusive terms to be responsible—not to this or that code, or cause, or creed—but to the reality these claim to serve and to the credentials of their claim. To protest, as history requires, that religions have been among the worst traitors to these meanings, is by the same token to affirm them as 'religious'.

If then, duly chastened and alerted, we can return to a religious denominator associating, however remotely, those who intend ultimate dimensions in their living and thinking, what is Christian mission to them?

It is so to live and relate that the symbol of the Christ is always available to be the clue for the yearnings of mankind. Those yearnings, as we have argued throughout, will necessarily spring from within the puzzles and exchanges of the common world and they will be generally tempered by the patterns of faith-systems already to hand. The calling of the Christian community is to be there with the Gospel as that sphere of association where the mystery is luminous. In art this means the ikon, the cross, the living face, the grace-cup and the broken bread. It does not mean the contemplative figure wrapped in meditative bliss. Nor does it mean the rivers of calligraphy, speaking a verbal education of mankind. Nor is it the lotus-flower of mysterious union. The Christian takes other religion to a babe in a manger and a man on a cross, to a holy table where bread and wine invite to fellowship in redemption. Our ambition is to have these always present to be the text of that search for expression which lies nearest to the heart of all human living, so that to feel, to suffer and to understand become one and the same thing.

Two examples are ready to hand. In his study of Christian Russia, James H. Billington, author of *The Icon and the Axe*,[14] describes how those two objects hung together on the wall of the peasant's hut in the rugged Russian north. Earth's timber and heaven's mercy, nature and man, work and worship. When, in Lenin's revolution, the face of the leader replaced the child and the madonna, *pravda*, or truth, became merely the title of a newspaper, with its absolute claims upon the spirit. There was still a ritual but the reverence was gone.

Or consider the Negro Spiritual as an art form. How many things come together in: 'Were you there when they crucified my Lord'? Biblical memory, western history, slave circumstance, implicit revolt, shared tragedy. But, since all these are emotionally set within the meaning of the Cross, there is a solidarity discovered which leaves sheer hatred behind, links itself with a paradigm of victory, and assures itself of peace in its meaning. It is by such a song that a mere submissive piety is transcended and that violent enmity is overcome. The celebration of a divine power at work in the world makes attitudes to a desperate situation not only religious, but what is more important, regenerative and blessed. 'Tell ole Pharaoh, let my people go', and 'Didn't my Lord deliver Daniel?' take the imagery further back, but Christianly. Such singing is not to be dismissed as merely compensatory. Rather it is faith living in its own landscape, as that landscape is given in the themes of Christ.

It has sometimes been observed that the Christian history owes as much to poetry as to fact, or rather the facts have blessedly engendered their own poetry—shepherds at Bethlehem, Mary and the angel, the Magi, and, most of all, the patterns of crucifixion. Supposedly if Jesus had been pushed over a cliff—as might have happened at Nazareth—or been made to drink hemlock in a Roman prison, we should not have found ourselves singing:

> See from his head, his hands, his feet,
> Sorrow and love flow mingling down,
> Did e'er such love and sorrow meet

Or thorns compose so rich a crown?

Yet, since the virtue lay in the will to suffer forgivingly, those other deaths would equally have redeemed mankind. God's mercy, however, allowed us the poetry as well. How eloquent that physical embrace, 'that one known human signature',[15] that 'line athwart another line' which is the human sign of the Cross. How large that token of the vulnerable, the open breast, the open palm. The crucified may not clench a defiant fist. The arts have every reason to take it to themselves. But it is the quality of the suffering that makes it so. Brush and poem interpret, but the Christ is the supreme original.

If things be thus are we not warranted in understanding our mission among the faiths as that of living with this artistry of men's forgiveness? Of ensuring that its meaning is there to seize upon wherever wistful spirits reach out for a text to make their vicissitudes religious? Of being instruments to that promise of the Lord: 'I will come to you'? There is no evangelism more sensitive, more apposite, than this.

And let us not forget the holy table of Jesus' own ordaining. Hospitality, as we argued in Chapter 2, has always been a tryst of men with men. Serving 'the Lord's table' is the most splendid diaconate. In the Church of Dominus Flevit on the western slopes of the Mount of Olives, one looks across the altar through the westward window to the holy city. In the iron grill of the window is the *motif* of the thorns and of the chalice and the paten. History and symbol are in one outline. This is the vocation of the Christian liturgy, 'spreading' as the psalmist has it 'a table before' men, hallowing in bread and wine the natural order, and 'showing forth the Lord's death' as the point of God's hospitality to the world. Then, 'in a far and humble likeness with the Lord's Supper', as Pasternak phrased it, we may offer ourselves to be Christ's broken bread among our fellows.

Other faiths, to be sure, have their symbolism, and for these our reverence and our study. But, in the Holy Spirit, the Babe, the Cross and the Eucharist are ours, not in vulgar competition, yet articulate and present, and always as an accusation of our own disloyalty.

I think of Giotto, the Tuscan shepherd's dream,
Christ . . .
How could our race betray
The Image, and the Incarnate One unmake,
Who chose this form and fashion for our sake?[16]

Edwin Muir's anxiety brings us to our second theme—the
Divine logic. With the expression in form goes the conception
in thought. Even the simple Joads had some reason in their
gesture. The principle of *Imitatio Christi*, which is deep in the
symbolic, has also to operate in the theological. The clues we
hold present for men in their imagination relate also to their
concepts. The Christian is committed to faith in the
Christlikeness of God because he believes in the divine nature
of Jesus as the Christ. This we have seen in Chapter 4. Love in
suffering as the heart of that divine nature therefore becomes
the central clue to our witness about the structures and powers
of the world.

Our sense of Jesus and the Cross, as the expression of the
divine mind, teaches us the partiality of all other means to the
good in history, evaluates and judges them and enables us to
find a policy toward them. Jesus' Messiahship within the mind
of God moves amid the options which variously represent the
decisions and powers of all human history. There is a national,
zealot Messiahship which, by its nature, is ethnically selective
and exclusive. There is the activist, political, militarist
Messiahship, which pays the price of violence and of necessity
excludes its enemies. There is the apocalyptic expectation
which is, again, selective and arbitrary, if not also impatient.
Or there is the view that essentially substitutes the community
and the law for the Messianic action. This must exclude the
outsider and the failure, the publican and the prodigal.

All these possible patterns of the kingdom are answers with
remainders. As revolutions, they are not revolutionary enough.
As compromises they are partial. As correctives they are
approximate. This is not to say that governments, law, politics
and nations do not have their place in the relativity of human
history. But the kingdom of God cannot be located in these. A
kingdom which identifies itself with one people, clings to

political sanction, marries with one cultural expression, stops short of the ultimate vocation. Only the Christic pattern retrieves the tragic situation of man. So it becomes for us the measure of the rule of God and so again, in turn, the criterion by which God himself is known.

In Jesus as the Christ we have, then, a logic which we can call divine by which to understand how the Holy Spirit would have us relate to the institutions of the state and of politics and of technology, to relate so as to hold them all liable to the human beyond the national, to the redemptive beyond the legal, to the spiritual beyond the political, to the eternal beyond the cultural. Just as 'the Son of Man had not where to lay his head', so his disciples must interpret the world and its crises in terms no less costly and compassionate than those which took their Master to Gethsemane.

That logic gives us to know that evil goes deeper than a particular economic system, without warranting us in blindly clinging to it. It makes all political and social solutions relative, without absolving us from the business of participation in them. It requires that we look beyond the nation to mankind without thereby escaping the immediacies of our own citizenship. It enables us to repudiate both the lovelessness of the Marxist dialectic and its utopian illusion of classless innocence, without failing to register its passionate rejection of the alienation of man. It allows us to measure the radical despair of the existentialists for whom God or 'Godot' never comes, without ceasing to trust the love that ever comes. It ranges us with every human perception of the sacred and invites it to deepen into the knowledge of grace as Christ offers it.

So much in religion turns upon the criteria by which we judge. Does our sense of impermanence and mortal flux warrant a Buddhist-style decision for the unreality of the personal dimension? Does a feeling of the inevitability of power equations in human history conduce to the Islamic pattern of religio-political unity in which faith and empire join? Does the seeming absence and silence of the divine leave us to assume that we are veritably on our own in the universe? Though elements of all these have found their place, sometimes a large place, in Christian history, the 'conclusion' Paul says we have come to (2 Cor. 5.14) because of Christ really disavows them all.

It is, then, this logic which, in the Holy Spirit, we commend to men and to the faiths in their history. But the final question lies with the will and here we face the most intimate area of our Christian duty to our fellow men—how to respect their autonomy as their Creator does—yet how to move them Christward in the freedom of their personal wills. The Joads, in our simple parable, had the impulse to make the burial 'religious'. Without that inward urge, reason and symbol would have had no place. True, text and idea were for them traditional and so could motivate the intention. But the urge came from wanting the dimension which quotation could express.

Here is the critical question for the Christian in the world—how to have the meanings of Christ operative in human hearts. 'The true understanding of Jesus', wrote Albert Schweitzer,

> . . . is the understanding of will acting on will. True relation to Him is to be taken possession of by Him.

Commenting on how pious people could not understand his decision for Africa and even thought it waste, Schweitzer continued:

> In the many verbal duels I had to fight, as a weary opponent, with people who passed for Christians, it moved me greatly to see them so far from perceiving that the effort to serve the love preached by Jesus may sweep a man into a new course of life, although they read in the New Testament that it can do so and find it quite in order.[17]

Perhaps it is that our Christianity is 'underdeveloped' in a deeper sense than that earlier cited from an Indian critic—'underdeveloped' not in its content but in its commitment, not in the range of its Christ but the reach of its Christians.

Clearly, it is the wills that are moved which move others. Schweitzer found his way to Africa via Bach's Chorales. The operating theatre in Lambaréné sprang from the organ stool in Strasbourg, and both from the meaning of Gethsemane. Whether through Scripture, music, compassion, companionship, symbol, eucharist or mind, it is the recruiting to Christ by Christ which is the heart of all Christian relating to mankind. 'Andrew first found his own brother Simon . . . and he brought him to Jesus' (John 1.41–2). Our task is to keep open to others every access within our power into those meanings where the will kindles into response. It is to serve the sensitivities whereby Jesus is known and received. It is to counter, as far as in us lies, what counters Christ, and yet to know that in the workings of his grace even the pre-empting prepossessions of other faiths may nevertheless prepare his way. Those prepossessions may not be impediments so long as they care about love. Dag Hammarskjöld, great Christian as he was, did not describe his will to faith in sharply exclusive terms.

I don't know Who—or what—put the question. I don't know when it was put. I don't even remember answering. But at some moment I did answer Yes to Someone—or Something—and from that hour I was certain that existence is meaningful and that, therefore, my life in self-surrender had a goal.[18]

It is better that such implicit discipleship should ripen into explicit faith in God through Christ than that articulate conviction should wither into barren orthodoxy or conforming unconcern.

But it is best of all if discipleship and conviction, the implicit and the explicit, sustain and energise each other. Or, as Hammarskjöld further prayed:

Thou who art over us,
Thou who art one of us,
Thou who *art*—
Also within us,
May all see Thee—in me also,
May I prepare the way for Thee,
May I thank Thee for all that shall fall to my lot,

May I also not forget the needs of others,
Keep me in Thy love
As Thou wouldest that all should be kept in mine.
May everything in this my being be directed to Thy glory
And may I never despair.
For I am under Thy hand,
And in Thee is all power and goodness.[19]

Such is the movement of the will to Christ. Its contagion in the daily world is our central hope and our prime vocation, grounded in the ever-present, ever-patient, Holy Spirit, Lord and giver of life.

Wrought in the historical and told in the conceptual, the Christian's faith is a poetry of the heart. And poetry, it has been said, never takes sides. Is there perhaps, at the end of the day, something rather disloyal that it should ardently want itself believed? Would it not be truer to its genius just to be there, blessedly for those who care, or can discern, but not insistently in search of discipleship? Does not doctrine, somehow, disserve poetry and, in seeking allegiance, forfeit sensitivity? 'Art', it has been said, 'abhors dogma . . .'

. . . imagination is curbed by the imperative need to believe, the need to proclaim in all its doctrinal purity the Gospel that saves. . . . The power of sensuous observation, uncensored insight into the complexities of the human soul . . . are gradually eliminated by the imagination as it hardens into the procrustean frame of dogmatic faith.[20]

We do not think so. On the contrary, the sensibilities of art decline into a register of spectacle[21] unless they are constantly recruited for the activity of being human. The poetry in the faith is the music of its will. Doctrine is the musical notation and the Christian is the instrumentalist. Does the poetry of the good Samaritan take no side in the situation? Shall we see his imagination curbed because he brings out the oil and the wine? And what is the source of the parable and its whole setting in Jesus but the oil and the wine of God? 'Go and do thou likewise' is, then, the final word, which is at once sign and logic, poetry and doctrine, rooted in

... the divine self-emptying from the foundation of the world. ... The believer is simply entering into a new and greatly deepened experience through Christ of what God has been doing all the time.[22]

Notes

PREFACE

[1] W. C. Smith, *The Meaning and End of Religion* (New York, 1st edn Macmillan, 1962; Mentor Books, 1964), p. 62. He adds: 'My objection to the term "Hinduism" . . . is not on the grounds that nothing exists. . . . My point . . . is that the mass of religious phenomena that we shelter under the umbrella of that term is not a unity and does not aspire to be.' This no one will deny. But we are in danger of a complete atomism if we insist that 'the Hindu' (assuming we designate at all) is totally and entirely peculiar to himself. Smith's concern is for the truth that 'Hinduism' is, diversely and always, 'Hindus' and not some abstraction. 'What have been called religions are at least the active and continuing responses of men' (p. 113).

CHAPTER 1

[1] The first sense of the question in Surah 56.58 is that the seed in human conception eludes the human eye. But in the other sense of the verb the text may be taken as a call to the awed reverence proper to the will for parenthood. In that most elemental of human capacities and the crux of all others, man is invited into wonder and thanksgiving.

[2] Louis Duprée, *The Other Dimension, A Search for the Meaning of Religious Attitudes* (New York: Doubleday, 1972), p. 31.

[3] Kofi Awoonor, *This Earth, My Brother* (London: Heinemann, 1972).

[4] John Ruskin, 'The Work of Iron in Nature, Art and Poetry', in *The Two Paths* (London: Allen, 1906), p. 202. Ruskin was addressing an audience in Tunbridge Wells in 1858. In lyrical vein, he extols iron, secret, as he sees it, alike of 'the crimson in the blood' and the colour in the landscape. Iron's very capacity to go rusty is a condition of its beneficence.

[5] Edited and introduced by Wilder Foote, *The Servant of Peace, A Selection of the Speeches and Statements of Dag Hammarskjöld* (London: The Bodley Head, 1962), pp. 160–1.

[6] Charles Davis in *Christ and the World Religions* (London: Hodder & Stoughton, 1970), p. 15, thinks the contrary when he writes: 'Systems of ultimate meaning are a matter of consumer preference, and quite a varied assortment is now available.' 'Religion . . . in the sphere of individual choice' would seem to be one thing, 'consumer preference' quite another. Certainly

our Christian witness, in the free-to-opt society, must be a sharing, not a selling, enterprise. And the deepest 'choosing' always regrets its rejecting.

[7] In *Cahiers Renaud-Barrault*, no. 23 (May 1958), p. 131. Quoted in Martin Esslin, *The Theatre of the Absurd* (London: Eyre & Spottiswoode, 1966), p. 298.

[8] Samuel Beckett, *Waiting for Godot* (London: Faber & Faber, 1951), p. 94:

Vladimir: 'Well? Shall we go?'
Estragon: 'Yes, let's go.' *They do not move.*
Curtain.

[9] Albert Camus, *Lyrical and Critical Essays*, edited by Philip Thody, trans. by E. C. Kennedy (New York: A. Knopf, 1970), p. 160.

[10] For example: Arend Van Leeuwen, *Christianity in World History*, trans. by H. H. Hoskins (London: Edinburgh House Press, 1964), pt viii, pp. 399–422.

[11] Martin Esslin, *op. cit.* note 7 above, pp. 301–2.

[12] Dietrich Bonhoeffer, *Letters and Papers from Prison* (3rd edn, rev.; London: SCM Press, 1967), p. 196.

[13] This, of course, is a main reason why W. C. Smith, in *The Meaning and End of Religion* (note 1, Preface), warns so strongly against thinking in set terms of the '-ism' (p. 23). Religions he sees as adjectives, secondary to persons, rather than as nouns. Where Smith seems to overstate his case is when he claims that each 'personal submittingness—if we may use such a term—is, of course, quite distinct from any other person's' (p. 107). I, speaking English, am unique: but the English I speak is not unique to me. Is it not more deeply so with faith than with language?

[14] Muhammad Iqbāl (1876–1938), foremost among modern thinkers in Indo-Pakistani Islam, published his *Lectures on a Reconstruction of Religious Thought in Islam*, in Lahore, 1933, and London, 1934 (Oxford University Press). He read ideas of creative evolution, like those of Henri Bergson, in the Qur'an, and by his vibrant poetry in Persian and Urdu strove to revitalise 'the caravan of Islam'.

[15] Charles Dickens, *Great Expectations* (London: Penguin edn, 1965), p. 311. Jaggers, the harsh lawyer, puzzling administrator of Pip's strange benefaction, and a tyrannising dispenser of 'the law's delays' and its cold heart.

CHAPTER 2

[1] Mai Mai Sze, *The Tao of Painting*, Bollinger series, xlix (London: Pantheon Books, 1956).

[2] I. C. Sharma, *Ethical Philosophies of India*, edited and revised by S. M. Daughert (London: George Allen & Unwin, 1965), pp. 298–9.

[3] Quoted in C. Humphreys, *The Wisdom of Buddhism* (new edn; London: Rider, 1970), p. 120.

[4] Martin Buber, *Two Types of Faith*, trans. by N. P. Goldhawk (London: Routledge & Kegan Paul, 1951), pp. 7–12. The type distinction pervades the

whole study, e.g. pp. 97–101 and 170 f. There are several times where the author modifies, even almost abandons, the rigour of his distinction, e.g. p. 11 and pp. 131, 132. 'Each of the two', he notes, 'has extended its roots into the other camp' (p. 11), and he is especially alive to the attraction of Francis of Assisi. The ruling typology, nevertheless, persists. Thus the meaning of Paul's 'end of the law for righteousness', and of the openness of the Church, is not seen. Faith *that*, 'proceeding from formula to formula and leading to the regular confession in creeds, belongs no longer in essence to living religion . . .' (p. 42).

⁵ Quoted in Ernst Simon, 'Martin Buber: his way between Thought and Deed', in *Jewish Frontier*, vol. 15 (February 1948) p. 26.

⁶ Leo Baeck, for example, sees in Christianity 'the quintessence of romanticism'. Cf. his *Judaism and Christianity*, trans. by W. Kaufmann (Philadelphia, 1958), p. 291, and *The Essence of Judaism* (Philadelphia, 1948), p. 13. See also Walter Jacob, *The Jewish Quarterly Review*, New York, vol. 56 (October, 1965), pp. 158–72.

⁷ Austin Farrer in *The Christian Understanding of Man*, a symposium, T. E. Jessup and others (London, George Allen & Unwin, 1938), p. 181.

⁸ In contradistinction to Kwama Nkrumah's 'Seek ye first the political kingdom . . . ' as the slogan of the Convention People's Party in Ghana in the fifties.

⁹ In *Hosties Noires*, trans. by John Reed and Clive Wake, *Prose and Poetry of Senghor* (London: Oxford University Press, 1965), pp. 134–6.

¹⁰ E. Berkovits, *Towards Historic Judaism* (1953). He says that under assimilation Jews had to pay with their souls for the tolerance they were granted. They were only given a reasonable chance of existence by consenting to 'wither away' as Jews. Finding statehood via Zionism was thus the only satisfactory shape of feasible religious existence. One should not have to pay for one's rights by risk of assimilation. Yet Berkovits also insists that 'every bit of this earth belongs to all of us who live on it', meaning that nations cannot require identity of belief or race as a condition of inhabiting it anywhere. Wherever people are they must not be merely there on sufferance. 'No country belongs to the majority that lives in it but to every human being living there.' At the same time Israel must exist to provide majority dominance for the Jewish people, as the indispensable condition of their religious continuity (*ibid*, pp. 138–9).

CHAPTER 3

¹ Quoted from Wellhausen, commenting on Matt. 6.9, by Martin Buber, *op. cit.* note 4 (Ch. 2 above), p. 157.

² In respect, for example, of Karl Barth's exclusive emphasis on divine initiative, it is probably wise to understand him as primarily affirming the inward experience of grace rather than denying the 'nighness of the word' in nature. As H. R. Mackintosh observes: 'He [Barth] is speaking of the Christian believer—not of the detached spectator, nor even of the anxious

enquirer—and elucidating that which, through the persuasion of the Holy Spirit, has become for *him* an irrefragable conviction. If I receive grace and thus perceive . . . that I am the object of God's pure compassion, for me the question is closed.' *Types of Modern Theology* (London: Nisbet & Co., 1937), p. 277.

³ Without the human seeking it is hard to see how revelation could ever happen. It is for this reason, among others, that we have to question the familiar distinction between Christianity and other faiths, according to which other faiths are men seeking God, while in Christianity it is God seeking man. The element of truth in this is much too neatly expressed. The divine seeking cannot be unilaterally confined, nor can the human seeking be excluded from the biblical experience. This will be clear from the whole pattern in Chapter 4 as a Christian *confessio fidei*.

⁴ Walter de la Mare, *Collected Poems* (London: Faber & Faber, 1969), pp. 754–5.

⁵ Gustav Janouch, *Conversations with Kafka*, trans. by Goronwy Rees (2nd edn; London: New Directions, 1971), p. 166.

⁶ *The Brothers Karamazov*, pt 2, ch. 3 (New York: Modern Library Edition, 1950), p. 279.

⁷ Franz Kafka, *The Penal Colony*, trans. by Willa and Edwin Muir (New York: Schocken Books, 1948), pp. 158–9.

⁸ *Samyutta Nikaya* iii, 83. Cf. *Concise Encyclopaedia of Living Faiths* edited by R. C. Zaehner (London: Hutchinson, 1959), 'Buddhism: The Theravada' by I. B. Horner, p. 293.

⁹ Thus, for example, in *The Concept of Man* edited by S. Radhakrishnan and P. T. Raju (London: Allen & Unwin, 1966), p. 247, Dr Raju observes: 'Of all the objects one's own body is chosen by the ego for identifying itself for the sake of activity and enjoyment', a view which hardly states the personal situation. Truly, we can think ourselves apart from our bodies but do we choose them from among other comparably available objects?

¹⁰ Cf. note 8 above. *Arhants* are those desireless ones who attain *Nirvana*.

¹¹ T. S. Eliot, *Four Quartets* (London: Faber & Faber, 1968 edn), 'Burnt Norton', p. 20.

¹² *Ibid.* p. 18.

¹³ Cf. His remark: 'The Upanishads . . . the greatest gift of this (19th) century." A. Schopenhauer: *The World as Will and Idea*, Vol. 3, p. 458, (London, 1888, Routledge & Kegan Paul.)

¹⁴ 'Europe swallowed up by Asia', was in fact the phrase used by Ignaz Maybaum, *Trialogue between Jew, Christian and Muslim* (London: Routledge and Kegan Paul, 1973), p. 41.

¹⁵ See *op. cit.* note 8 above, p. 306, where E. Conze writes of the 'historical Buddha' in 'fictitious' body dwelling in saints to aid the needy: 'The idea is not unlike that of St Paul who claimed that it was not he who spoke but the Christ who spoke in him.'

¹⁶ Cf. *op. cit.* note 8 above, p. 296. E. Conze notes that the rise of the Mahayana coincides with the beginning of the Christian era, and adds: 'This raises an interesting, and so far unresolved, historical problem', namely the

possible influence of Christian parallels in compassion/love, in Bodhisattvas/Christ grace, and in eschatology. See also R. L. Slater, *World Religions and World Community* (New York: Columbia University Press, 1963), ch. 4.

[17] Though that dichotomy need not be stated so sharply as R. C. Zaehner does in the title, and content, of his *Mysticism, Sacred and Profane* (London: Oxford University Press, 1961 edn).

[18] See E. H. Whinfield's translation of Shabastari's *Gulshan i Raz*, Mahmud ibn 'Abd al-Karim Shabistari: *Gulshan-i-Raz*, edit. by E. H. Whinfield (London, 1880, Trübner & Co.) p. 46.

[19] The poet Jami in *Yusuf and Zulaikha*, in E. G. Browne, *Literary History of Persia* (Cambridge, 1928), vol. 1, pp. 439 and 442.

[20] See discussion in this writer's *The Wisdom of the Sufis* (London: Sheldon, 1976), in relation to the tenth-century mystic Al Junaid and the sixteenth-century Al Sirhindi, both of whom, along with many other Islamic mystical writers, employed in varying ways the twin metaphors of inebriate sobriety.

[21] A. J. Arberry, trans., *The Ruba'iyyat of Jalal al Din Rumi* (London: Emery Walker), p. 29.

[22] 'Saul' in *The Poetical Works of Robert Browning* (London: Oxford University Press, 1940 edn), p. 231.

[23] Miguel de Unamuno, *The Tragic Sense of Life in Men and Nations*, trans. by Anthony Kerrigan (London: Routledge & Kegan Paul, 1972), p. 211.

CHAPTER 4

[1] *The Poems of Robert Herrick*, edited by L. C. Martin (London: Oxford University Press, 1965), pp. 398–9: 'Good Friday; *Rex Tragicus*, Christ going to His Cross.'

[2] Peter Brook, *The Empty Space* (London: MacGibbon & Kee, 1968).

[3] *Ibid.*, p. 56.

[4] A. Loisy, *The Birth of the Christian Religion*, trans. L. P. Jacks (London: George Allen and Unwin, 1948). See Chap. III.

[5] R. C. Moberly, *Atonement and Personality* (London: John Murray, 1901), pp. 322–3.

[6] This whole theme is the subject of the companion volume by the editor of Mowbray's Library of Theology, i.e. Michael Perry, *The Ressurrection of Man* (London: Mowbrays, 1975).

[7] One example among several authors would be Herschel Baker, *The Image of Man* (New York: Harper Bros, 1947 and 1961), who readily attributes the entire New Testament understanding of the divinity and death of Jesus and of the Eucharist to pagan influences. In his estimate it is, indeed, the influences which are in fact the origins.

CHAPTER 5

[1] *Rudyard Kipling's Verse*, the definitive edition (London: Hodder &

Stoughton, 1940), p. 445: 'The Mother Lodge.'

[2] A pointed example of such tasks is studied in *Beyond Tolerance*, edited by Michael Hurley (London: Geoffrey Chapman, 1975). Sub-titled *The Challenge of Mixed Marriage* it deals with the issues of interfaith marriage, with particular reference to the problems involved in Ireland. There are two papers in a wider context by Fr Adrian Hastings and the present writer.

[3] B. Chaturvedi and M. Sykes, *The Life of C. F. Andrews* (New York: Harper Bros, 1950), p. 102, in a letter from Andrews to Rabindranath Tagore.

[4] *Ibid.*, p. 111. In a letter to Tagore.

[5] *Ibid.*, p. 310. In a letter to Gandhi.

[6] *Ibid.*, p. 65. In a Preface to the *Collected Writings of Swami Rama Tirtha*.

[7] *Ibid.*, p. 235. In a pamphlet published by the Society of Friends with the title, *Why I am a Christian*.

[8] Karl Barth, *The Epistle to the Romans*, trans. by Edwin C. Hoskyns (London: Oxford University Press, 1933), p. 96.

[9] *Ibid.*, p. 38.

[10] Herbert Butterfield, *Christianity and History* (London: G. Bell & Sons, 1949), p. 146. It may be useful to cite here C. F. Andrews's ardent, yet surely naïve remarks, '. . . to empty ourselves of the west, to be citizens of no country, but Christians, pure and simple, like the first disciples'. Are there feasibly any Christians, Muslims, or whatever, 'pure and simple'? Each, to start with, will have a mother tongue. For Andrews, see *op. cit.* p. 73.

[11] Hendrik Kraemer, *The Christian Message in a Non-Christian World* (London: Edinburgh House Press, 1938), p. 122.

[12] *Ibid.*, p. 123.

[13] *Ibid.*, p. 123.

[14] London: Oxford University Press, 1913.

[15] London: Lutterworth Press, 1960, pp. 375–6. Kraemer's other large work in this field was *Religion and the Christian Faith* (London: Lutterworth Press, 1956).

[16] The phrasing is that of *World Mission Report of the United Church of Canada* (Toronto, 1966), p. 137. See also Wilfred Cantwell Smith in *The Church in the Modern World*, edited by G. Johnstone and W. Roth (Toronto: Ryerson Press, 1967), pp. 154–70.

[17] *Loc. cit.* note 11 above, p. 120.

[18] David A. Brown, *A New Threshold* (London: British Council of Churches, 1976), pp. 21, 23.

[19] *Ibid.*, p. 23.

[20] Professor John H. Hick in a privately published paper. See also *The Expository Times*, Edinburgh, vol. 84, no. 2 (November 1972), pp. 36–9. See also D. B. Forrester's reply to Hick in *The Scottish Journal of Theology*, vol. 29, pp. 65–72: 'Professor Hick and the Universe of Faiths.'

[21] W. B. Yeats, *Autobiographies* (London: Macmillan, 1955), p. 468.

[22] William Ernest Hocking, *Living Religions and a World Faith* (New York: Macmillan, 1940), pp. 198–9.

[23] *Ibid.*, p. 199.

[24] See, for example, Winston L. King, *Buddhism and Christianity: Some Bridges of Understanding* (Philadelphia: Westminster Press, 1962), p. 227.

[25] Bishop Khodr's Paper was circulated within the WCC Central Committee.

[26] This theme is more fully handled in my *Christianity in World Perspective* (London: Lutterworth, 1968), ch. 2, pp. 40–63.

[27] John Sargent, *Memoir of Henry Martyn* (London, 1816), p. 107; and George Wilberforce, editor, *Journals and Letters of Henry Martyn* (London, 1837), vol. 2, p. 252.

[28] Marco Pallis, *Peaks and Llamas* (London: Cassell & Co., 1939), Chap. xi.

CHAPTER 6

[1] Seyyid Hossein Nasr, *Islam and the Plight of Modern Man* (London: Longman Group, 1976).

[2] Among them *Ideals and Realities of Islam* (London: George Allen & Unwin, 1966); *The Encounter of Man and Nature* (London: George Allen & Unwin, 1968); *Islamic Studies* (Beirut: Librairie du Liban, 1967).

[3] *Op. cit.* note 1 above, p. xi.

[4] *Ibid.*, pp. 4, 5 and 7.

[5] S. Kierkegaard, *Purity of Heart is to Will One Thing,* trans. by D. Steere (London: Collins, Fontana edn, 1961).

[6] Robert Browning, *loc. cit.* n. 22, ch. 3, 'Bishop Blougram's Apology', p. 444:

> What think ye of Christ, friend? when all's done and said,
> Like you this Christianity or not?
> It may be false, but will ye wish it true?
> Has it your vote to be so if it can?

[7] Quoted in C. M. Bowra, *Poetry and Politics 1900–1960* (London: Cambridge University Press, 1966), p. 139.

[8] Arthur C. Danto, *Mysticism and Morality* (London: Penguin, 1976), p. 81.

[9] John Oman, *Grace and Personality* (London: Collins, Fontana edn, 1960), p. 68.

[10] Cf. John Wild in the Centennial Lectures at the American University of Beirut, 1966, published in Charles Malik, *God and Man in Contemporary Christian Thought* (Beirut, 1970), pp. 74–5.

[11] Perhaps the first words were: 'You turned to God from idols . . .' (1 Thess. 1.9). Gilbert Murray will hardly be thought a partial witness. In his *Stoic, Christian and Humanist* (London: Watts, 1940), he notes on pp. 84 f. how the very survival of philosophy in the Graeco-Roman world owes much to the Christian rescue of the mind from the tyranny of multiplied deities. Minucius Felix's dialogue *Octavius* is quoted by Murray as evidence of the way in which Christian faith liberated an educated man from ancient superstitions.

[12] Among them, *An Invitation to Sociology, A Humanist Perspective* (London: Pelican, 1966); and *The Social Reality of Religion* (London, Penguin, 1967).

[13] *A Rumour of Angels* (London: Pelican, 1969), p. 96.

[14] In *The Church Looks Forward* (London: Macmillan, 1944, p. 71) he used the phrase at the end of a lecture on 'The Church's Approach to the Problem of Venereal Disease'.

[15]   Most like an arch: two weaknesses that lean
            Into a strength. Two failings become firm.
            Two joined abeyances become a term
            Naming the fact which teaches fact to mean.

[16] Martin Buber, *Israel and the World, Essays in a Time of Crisis* (New York: Schocken Books, 1963 edn), pp. 190–1.

[17] *Ibid.*, p. 178.

[18] Rabbi Lionel Blue (*To Heaven with Scribes and Pharisees*, London, 1975), remarks of Christians: 'For them the Unknowable has a birth certificate and people ... shared a meal with the Infinite. ... But Jews have a harder task' (p. 62).

CHAPTER 7

[1] John Steinbeck, *The Grapes of Wrath* (New York: Viking Press, 1939 ed), p. 170.

[2] *The Treatise of the Apostolic Tradition of St Hippolytus of Rome*, edited by Gregory Dix (London: SPCK, 1968), 21.17 and 22.1, i.e. pp. 37 and 38.

[3] Cf. J. E. Fison, in *The Blessing of the Holy Spirit* (London: Longmans Green, 1950), pp. 146–7. 'St John limits the work of the Holy Spirit to the Church and only through the Church can the Holy Spirit influence the world. This sharp delimitation of the frontiers of His operations stands out in glaring contrast to our easy-going way of speaking of His universal work.'

[4] Quoted in Mark Schorer, *William Blake: The Politics of Vision* (New York: Henry Holt, 1959), p. 20.

[5] See, for example, the illuminating study in Klaus Klostermaier, *Hindu and Christian in Vrindaban* (London: SCM Press, 1969).

[6] *Ibid.*, p. 29.

[7] *Complete Prose Works of John Milton* (London: Oxford University Press, 1949), vol. 2, pp. 235–6.

[8] *Christian Believing*, London, SPCK, 1976. The phrase is the title of Chapter 2.

[9] *Ibid.*, p. 5.

[10] *Ibid.*, p. 12.

[11] *Ibid.*, p. 42.

[12] Barth's repudiation of empirical religious systems as expressive of the fallenness of man, as well as the growing modern idea that theism is really infantile and an incubus on the sort of human autonomy which technology exercises, all these, and other factors, have encouraged the idea of

religionlessness, of deconsecration of nature, of man required to live without God in the world. See, *inter alia*: Arend Van Leeuwen, *Christianity in World History* (London: Lutterworth Press, 1964); Harvey Cox, *The Secular City* (London: Macmillan, 1965); John A. T. Robinson, *Honest to God* (London: SCM Press, 1963); D. Bonhoeffer, *Letters and Papers from Prison*, edited by E. Bethge (London: Collins, 1953). For some evaluation see this writer's *Christianity in World Perspective* (London, Lutterworth Press, 1968), ch. 7.

[13] T. S. Eliot, *Murder in the Cathedral* (London: Faber & Faber, 1935 edn), p. 48.

[14] James H. Billington, *The Icon and the Axe* (New York: Random House, 1962).

[15] From a poem, 'Cruciform', by Winifred Welles. See *Poems of our Time, 1900–1960*, edited by R. Church and M. Bozman (London: Dent, 1959), p. 295:

> Here, in one line athwart another line,
> Is briefly written the one mutual name,
> A saviour's, or a thief's, or yours, or mine.

[16] Edwin Muir, *Collected Poems* (London: Faber & Faber, 1952), from the poem, 'The Incarnate One', beginning: 'The windless northern surge. . . .'

[17] Albert Schweitzer, *My Life and Thought: An Autobiography,* trans. by C. T. Campion (London: Allen & Unwin, 1933), pp. 71, 108.

[18] Dag Hammarskjöld, *Markings*, trans. by L. Sjoberg and W. H. Auden (New York: A. Knopf, 1964), p. 205.

[19] *Ibid.*, p. 100.

[20] Charles I. Glicksberg, *Modern Literature and the Death of God* (The Hague: Martinus Nijhoff, 1966), p. 72.

[21] As, for example, in Somerset Maugham, *A Summing Up* (London), where he expounds the spectator attitude of the artist (as he sees him): 'Everything is grist to his mill, from the glimpse of a face in the street to a war that convulses the civilized world, from the scent of a rose to the death of a friend. Nothing befalls him that he cannot transmute into a stanza, a song or a story and having done this to be rid of it' (pp. 185–6).

[22] H. Wheeler Robinson, *Redemption and Revelation* (London, Nisbet & Co., 1942), p. 295.

Glossary of terms

(see Index for References)

Advaita: Non-duality, the totality of partless, undifferentiated reality: the essential identity of all that is.

Allah: The Arabic Qur'anic term: God. It is best so translated and not Anglicised. In English speech the strongly doubled 'l' consonants and the emphatic, long second syllable are lost. In derivation it probably is Al-Ilah: 'the God'. Incapable of plural.

Anatta: A Pali word (Sanskrit: anatman), the unselfed: the not-self: when personal individuation, or soul, is denied and a state of non-individual, identity-lessness is attained. The fiction that there is any permanent ego.

Arhant: (or Arahant). A Pali word (Sanskrit: Arhat). One who has become enlightened by the fourfold path of Theravada Buddhism: the initiate of the Hinayana ascetic discipline.

Atman: The individual soul. Identical with Brahman, though the fact of such identity has to be realised beyond the illusions of this transient world. Or the supreme transcendent spirit.

Avatara: An incarnation of, for example, Vishnu, in various forms, perhaps ten in all. Descent, or manifestation, of the Real to succour the human condition.

Bhagavad Gita: 'The Song of the Lord', *c.* second century BC, part of the great Hindu epics or Mahabharata. The most popular of all Hindu Scriptures.

Bhakti: A Sanskrit term denoting a pattern of devotion to a personified ideal or idea: a discipline of love to a personalised deity in Hinduism: a form of yogic discipline.

Bismillah: The invocation in Islam: 'In the Name of the merciful Lord of mercy', incorporating the first pair in the ninety-nine Names of God.

Bodhisattvas: (Sanskrit) (Pali: Bodhisattas). In Mahayana Buddhism those who have attained bliss but avail to illuminate the human scene: embodiments of the ageless Buddha in dedication to the service of mankind: the goodness of the Buddha personified.

brahma: (masculine). The creator in Hindu mythology.

Brahman: (neuter). Ultimate Reality, infinite and absolute beyond all phenomena, all form and all apprehension: impersonal World-Spirit. The concept has roots in the sacrifice notion of holy power of sacredness in the Upanishads. The sacred force present in religious acts lies behind all phenomena (cf. brahmanas, or cultic priests, brahmins).

deva: A Sanskrit term meaning either a god or for example in the later Upanishads, God in theistic sense.

Dhammapada: (Pali). An important Buddhist Scripture, a collection of aphorisms inculcating dharma.

dharma: (Sanskrit) (Pali: Dhamma). The most fundamental term in Hinduism and Buddhism. Means religion, duty, the teaching, the social order, the right way, or the norm. It is the teaching of the Buddha, or the path of preordained doing commanded in the Gita.

Din: The inclusive Islamic term, meaning religion, responsive to Iman, meaning faith. That which is due, is done, in response to God in revelation.

dukkha: (Pali). The suffering, or grief, that arise from impermanence and decay, the pain and forlornness of all living things.

emunah: Hebrew faithfulness or fidelity, the trustfulness and obedience that respond to the divine trust-keeping in history and the covenant.

fana': An Arabic term used in Sufism to denote the passing away of the empirical self in the state of absorption into God (see Tauhid).

fitrat Allah: Surah 30.30, in the Qur'an, reads: 'The nature of God on which He has natured man.' A basic concept in Islamic thought: man as conformable to the divine design.

Ishvara: (Sanskrit: the Lord). A term with several meanings in Hinduism. An object of meditative devotion, the creator Lord who creates the unreal universe, the emanation of absolute Brahman, or identifiable with the latter *qua* worship but never *qua* essence.

islam: The small 'i' is appropriate: Islam, the historic religion, is understood as embodying the final form of something much older, namely due submission or subordination to God.

Jahiliyyah: The state of ignorance, and unruliness or uncouthness which preceded the rise of Islam in Arabia and the light of the Qur'an.

jiva: The soul, or life monad, as understood in some Hindu usage.

karma: From the Sanskrit verb: to act (Pali: kamma). The necessary entail of the past, the law of continuity of effect, the momentum of deeds through the succession of rebirths.

muslim: Note the small 'm' as under islam. The muslim is the one who submits to God. The term is descriptive of, for example, Adam, Abraham, Jesus, etc., before its meaning is finalised and formalised in the faith of the Muslims.

Nirvana: Sanskrit term (Pali: Nibbana). The ultimate bliss of enlightenment in which dukkha is overcome, all separatedness is lost in the not-born, the not-becoming, the not-desiring.

pistis: The Greek New Testament term for faith, receiving for true and trusting for real.

Qur'an: The Islamic Scripture; literally the recital, the heavenly Scripture uttered and recorded and recited on earth.

samsara: (Sanskrit and Pali). The world of flux and transience, of being and becoming, life in the illusion of selfhood, all that awaits Nirvana.

Shahadah: The Muslim's witness that 'There is no god but God and Muhammad is His apostle'. The first pillar of Din in Islam.

Shariah: The sacred Law in Islam, literally the path. Derived from the Qur'an, Tradition, Analogy and Consensus, the first named being regulative.

Shirk: The most heinous of sins in Islam: alienating to pseudo-gods or loyalties the worship, submission, trust, and hope properly due to God alone. To commit idolatry.

Takbir: The ascription of greatness to God in Islam: saying: Allahu akbar, as in the call to prayer and personal devotion and Sufi liturgy. The form akbar is comparative, but nothing is worthy to enter the comparison.

Tanha: A Pali word meaning the drive, or craving to be, the urge to exist and desire which must be abated.

Tathagata: A teacher or enlightened one, a Buddha.

Tat tvam asi: Three Sanskrit words which embody the Hindu religion: That Thou art.

Tauhid: The affirmation, in Islam, that God is One: the inclusive sovereignty of God over all. In Sufism the term becomes synonymous with the unitive state, or ecstatic union.

Upanishads: Hindu Scriptures originating between 800 and 600 BC. The last of the Vedas or Sruti Scriptures.

Vedanta: 'The end of the Vedas', the teaching of Sankara being the most notable of all, whose central tenet was the passing away of individuality into boundless being.

vidya: Sanskrit term meaning knowledge, awareness, conditional upon detachment and meditation leading to insight. The knowing that is the unknowing of illusion: the Hindu salvation.

Index